Globalization and
Global Governance

CHATHAM HOUSE PAPERS

An International Economics Programme Publication
Programme Head: Dr Brigitte Granville

The Royal Institute of International Affairs, at Chatham House in London, has provided an impartial forum for discussion and debate on current international issues for nearly 80 years. Its resident research fellows, specialized information resources, and range of publications, conferences, and meetings span the fields of international politics, economics, and security. The Institute is independent of government.

Chatham House Papers are short monographs on current policy problems which have been commissioned by the RIIA. In preparing the papers, authors are advised by a study group of experts convened by the RIIA, and publication of a paper indicates that the Institute regards it as an authoritative contribution to the public debate. The Institute does not, however, hold opinions of its own; the views expressed in this publication are the responsibility of the author.

CHATHAM HOUSE PAPERS

Globalization and Global Governance

Vincent Cable

THE ROYAL INSTITUTE
OF INTERNATIONAL
AFFAIRS

Pinter
A Cassell imprint
Wellington House, 125 Strand, London WC2R 0BB
370 Lexington Avenue, New York, NY 10017-6550

First published in 1999

© Royal Institute of International Affairs, 1999–10-08

British Library Cataloguing-in-Publication Data
A CIP catalogue record for this book is available from the British Library.

Library of Congress Cataloging-in-Publication Data
A CIP catalogue record for this book is available from the Library of Congress.

ISBN 1-85567-351-7 (paperback)
1-85567-350-9 (hardback)

Typeset by Koinonia Limited
Printed and bound in Great Britain by
Biddles Limited, Guildford and King's Lynn

For Olympia

Contents

Contents

Foreword

Globalization is a term so widely used that its significance seems to be lost in endless partisan battles. The task that Vincent Cable has undertaken in this book is to offer a *tour d'horizon* of the issues involved – first definitional, followed by a comprehensive discussion hinging on the related questions of whether globalizing processes in various forms and fields are inevitable, and if so desirable. Cable brings to this discussion an illuminating twin perspective: an economic analysis of the rationale and benefits of globalization, combined with a political sensitivity to the reactions, often negative, which globalization provokes. This approach leads to perhaps the most important conclusion: that globalizing processes need regulation capable of protecting the resulting benefits from the opinion-mobilizing enemies of globalization comprising 'nationalists, mercantilists, regionalists, dependency theorists and deep greens'.

I am happy to declare a personal interest in arranging for the publication of this book by the Royal Institute of International Affairs. I have long missed a single comprehensive survey and authoritative discussion of the various issues and effects – both good and bad – of globalization, and I knew that Vincent Cable could fill that gap on my reference bookshelves.

Dr Brigitte Granville
Head, International Economics Programme
Royal Institute of International Affairs

Acknowledgments

I would like to thank former colleagues at Chatham House for encouraging this project which started when I was Head of the International Economics Programme (IEP). Particular thanks are due to Professor David Henderson, then chair of the IEP Advisory Board; Dr Brigitte Granville, current Head of Programme; Margaret May for editorial support; and Fionnuala O'Flynn, Joann Fong and Matthew Link for work on the text.

I received valuable insights from long discussions on the book with Albert Bressand of Prométhée, in Paris – indeed, at one stage it was to be a joint project; also from my former colleagues at Shell while I was Chief Economist there – especially Roger Rainbow and Ged Davis, Head of Planning.

I must acknowledge too the help of my much-loved wife, Olympia, without whose moral support, patience and encouragement I would never have completed the book amid the many claims on an MP's time.

October 1999   V.C.

About the author

Dr Vincent Cable is currently MP for Twickenham, and Liberal Democrat Spokesman on Trade and Industry. He was previously Chief Economist with Shell International; Special Professor of International Economics at the University of Nottingham; Head of the International Economics Programme at the Royal Institute of International Affairs; Special Adviser to John Smith when he was Secretary of State for Trade and Industry; Special Adviser to Sir Sridath Ramphal when he was Commonwealth Secretary General; and Deputy Director of the Overseas Development Institute.

Abbreviations

APEC	Asia-Pacific Economic Community
ASEAN	Association of South-East Asian Nations
BCCI	Bank of Credit and Commerce International
BIS	Bank for International Settlements
BJP	Bharatiya Janata Party (India)
CDMA	Code Division Multiple Access
CEN	European Committee for Standardization
CENELEC	European Committee for the Coordination of Electrical Standards
CFCs	chlorofluorocarbons
COCOM	Coordinating Committee for Multilateral Export Controls
COMECON	Council for Mutual Economic Assistance
DAC	Development Advisory Committee (of the OECD)
ECB	European Central Bank
ECOSOC	European Economic and Social Committee
EMU	Economic and Monetary Union
ETSI	European Telecommunications Standards Institute
FDI	foreign direct investment
GAAP	Generally Accepted Accounting Principles
GATT	General Agreement on Tariffs and Trade
GDP	gross domestic product
GII	global information infrastructure
GSM	Global System Mobile
IAIS	International Association of Insurance Supervisors
IAS(C)	International Accounting Standards (Committee)
ICAO	International Civil Aviation Organization

Abbreviations

ICC	International Chambers of Commerce
ICFTU	International Confederation of Free Trade Unions
IEC	International Electro-technical Commission
IIF	Institute of International Finance
IMF	International Monetary Fund
IOSCO	International Organization of Securities Commissions
ISO	International Organization for Standardization
ITU	International Telecommunications Union
LNG	liquefied natural gas
MAI	Multilateral Agreement on Investment
MIGA	Multilateral Investment Guarantee Agency
NAFTA	North American Free Trade Agreement
OECD	Organization for Economic Cooperation and Development
OFTEL	Office of Telecommunications
OPEC	Organization of Oil Exporting Countries
R&D	research and development
SEC	Securities and Exchange Commission
TDMA	Time Division Multiple Access
TRIMS	(GATT/WTO Agreement on) Trade-related Investment Measures
TRIPS	(GATT/WTO Agreement on) Trade-related Intellectual Property Rights
UNEP	United Nations Environment Programme
UNCITRAL	United Nations Commission on International Trade Law
VER	voluntary export restraint
UNCTAD	United Nations Conference on Trade and Development
UNIDO	United Nations Industrial Development Organization
WHO	World Health Organization
WMO	World Meteorological Organization
WTO	World Trade Organization

Chapter 1

The state of globalization

Globalization is one of the central concepts in current analysis of the economy and society. The term was first used 40 years ago – with a reference in the *Economist* – but the idea of modernization within a global market-place has much earlier origins in the writings of Saint-Simon and Marx. The financial crisis which spread through emerging markets in 1998 brought home to many people the extent to which their livelihood depends on unpredicable events a long way away. It now seems likely that, while deeply traumatic for many individuals and some countries, notably Asia and the former Soviet Union, this latest crisis will prove to have been no more than one of the growing pains of an increasingly interdependent global economic system. There have been panic and warnings of imminent collapse before: in the early 1970s with the demise of the Bretton Woods fixed exchange-rate regime; in the late 1970s after the OPEC 'oil shock' and with worries about 'the world running out of raw materials'; in the early 1980s with the Latin American debt crisis and fears for the solvency of major Western banks; and in 1987, with an equity market collapse in the US.

It is still possible – though unlikely – that bad luck and incompetence could turn recent signs of systemic weaknesses into a collapse of the kind experienced in the wake of the 1929 crash. But, even if it does not, there is a proper questioning of globalization and the system of governance on which economic integration is based. This volume seeks to address some of these issues: what does globalization mean? Is it inevitable? And, if not, is it desirable? How does 'the system' – the present network of formal and informal rules and institutions – actually work? What are the major gaps and deficiencies? What would be a practical agenda for international economic policy reform?

Globalization: what does it mean?

In the vast, multidisciplinary literature that has multiplied rapidly during the 1990s (Held et al., 1999; Waters, 1995), 'globalization' has become a portmanteau term – of description, approval or abuse – referring to many different things. There is a perception, and often a reality, of globally integrated systems of physical communication (telephony; the Internet; airline networks); shared entertainment (film and TV; popular and classical music; sport); economic exchange and capital flows; and the accelerating spread of ideas and of competing spiritual values (through evangelical Christianity and Islam).

Keniichi Ohmae's phrase, 'the borderless world', captures the sense of radical progress and modernity, and of life beyond the constraints of the traditional nation-state, which infuses much of the popular writing about 'globalization' (Ohmae, 1990). Certainly the concept has meaning for those in senior management positions, in growing innovative companies, Internet users, communications specialists, frequent business travellers and those sufficiently qualified or affluent to move freely, shop around and invest in a multiplicity of markets. It is manifested in common tastes, common technical and performance standards, common ideas of 'best practice', common language (English and the main software packages) and easy, rapid communications.

The concept of globalization is not just descriptive, it is also normative. Many relish the excitement and the widening of opportunities and want to remove barriers to markets and mobility. But others are alarmed by real or imagined threats to their identity or the ability of their governments to exercise control over events. There is now a variety of separate battlegrounds where these competing ideas are at odds: trade and immigration policy (in the US and France, for example); attitudes to foreign enterprises (in India and Russia); freedom of access to offensive or threatening material on the Internet (in the US and Singapore) or satellite television (in China). The financial crisis and slump in 1998 in Asia and Russia has focused attention on the issue of how far governments can or should regulate short-term capital flows and may well broaden out into a deeper questioning of economic openness. There are numerous tracts, pressure groups and parties advocating some variant of

2

'new' (but usually rather old) protectionism. I am hostile to protectionism in any guise and believe in the benefits of global economic integration. But the critics have to be answered; they cannot just be assumed away.

Many analysts have, moreover, begun to question the extent and permanence of the globalization process. The critique has three elements. The first is that in some respects globalization is not well advanced, falling well short of complete global integration and even less advanced than in earlier periods of history: as Martin Wolf recently put it, 'if not a myth, a huge exaggeration' (Wolf, 1998). The second is that integration is not irreversible and has been reversed before. The third is that the role of nation-state institutions is far from redundant, though there may have been changes in the way national governments can exercise sovereignty.

We shall try here to advance the discussion by deconstructing the various separate elements which make up the globalization phenomenon. This is not a straightforward task. Different disciplines employ different criteria. Geographers have drawn heavily on physical measures which alter the relationship between space and time: the impact of falling transport barriers, progressing from the 10 mph average of stagecoaches and ships in the world before 1850 to the speeds of jet aircraft in the 1960s (Dicken, 1992); from the days of hand-borne messages, through the nineteenth-century revolution of telephony including intercontinental calls, to today's world where there is a variety of telecommunications transmission mechanisms with instant global link-ups and close to zero marginal cost.

The economist's perspective, adopted here, takes as a reference point the idea of globalization as a model of fully internationally integrated markets, defined by David Henderson (1999) as those meeting two conditions:

- free movement of goods, services, labour and capital: thus a single market in inputs and outputs;
- full national treatment for foreign investors (and nationals working overseas) so that, economically speaking, there are no foreigners.

The ultimate consequence of such a world would be the equalization of prices – and returns to capital and labour – the 'law of one price' – subject to differences in quality and transport. We are clearly very far from such a world, though different parts are integrated to different degrees across and within countries. Although the EU is legally, and increasingly in practice, a single market, some large countries are not: China has restrictions on internal migration; India has taxes and controls on inter-state trade; Canada and the US tolerate substantial limitations of freedom of internal trade, or distortions of it. Nowhere is there anything approximating to free labour movement across frontiers. Nonetheless there has clearly been a progression towards the conditions in the theoretical model. While I work principally with a – usually – implicit model of economic integration, this begs difficult questions about what 'national' and 'foreign' mean. It is not immediately obvious what a 'British company' or even a British person actually is: both involve complicated and changing definitions based on residence, tax status, citizenship, blood ties and identity.

Another way of characterizing globalization is through a mixture of legal and organizational categories. Richard O'Brien, in his *End of Geography* (1992), has helpfully made the following distinctions:

- purely *domestic*, national, activities.
- *international* (or cross-border) activities involving sales of goods and services, financial flows or movements of people across frontiers.
- *multinational* activities involving operations in more than one country at once. Multinational companies operating in several countries can incorporate different combinations of multiple domestic business and/or international cross border business.
- *offshore* activities – those outside a specific national jurisdiction.
- *global* activities, which are qualitatively different from those that are international, multinational or offshore. The term suggests a different degree of integration and coordination. Customers can be offered a global service, wherever they are, and production can be organized with little regard to national frontiers.

Globalization essentially refers to a mixture of international, multinational, offshore and global activities and involves a general progression from the domestic to the global.

Deconstructing globalization

The first step is to look at what is actually going on. The broad picture is clear: world trade in goods and services, foreign direct investment and increased financial flows all suggest growing interdependence (Figure 1.1). The different components of globalization tell a more varied story.

In relation to *trade* it is possible to measure meaningfully the extent of

Figure 1.1: Integration of the world economy during the 1990s

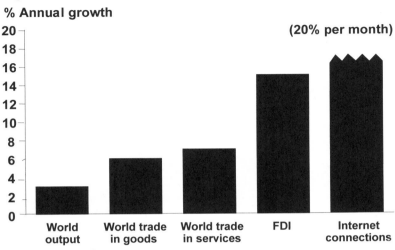

% Annual growth

(20% per month)

World output | World trade in goods | World trade in services | FDI | Internet connections

Source: GATT/WTO.

globalization – or economic integration – by contrasting the growth of trade with the growth of output. Throughout the postwar period world trade has grown more rapidly than output in volume terms. In aggregate terms the share of trade in global output has increased from around 7% in 1950 to over 20% today (Maddison, 1995). The significance of this conclusion has to be qualified in several ways.

First, it is not a totally new phenomenon. Before the First World War the same process occurred. Indeed in 1913 the degree of openness for many countries was much as it is today (Figure 1.2). This is true even of major trading countries like the US and Japan. There are measurement problems when it comes to openness but there seems little doubt as to the overall conclusion that there is nothing historically unique about current levels of trade integration: history also suggests that nothing is irreversible. Second, the rapid growth of trade (relative to output) has been in manufactures (and, even more, in traded services). It is not true of agriculture (because of numerous restrictions on trade) or raw materials (because there were few restrictions to remove). And, third, a major part of the growth of world trade has occurred within regions rather than between them. In particular, if the internal trade of the EU is treated as 'national' – within a Single Market – rather than international, the process of global integration looks decidedly less impressive.

5

Figure 1.2: Share of exports as percentage of GDP

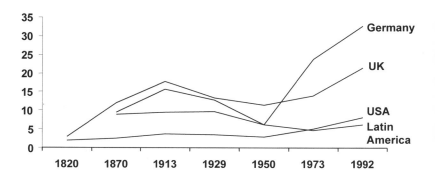

Source: Maddison, 1995.

Trade growth has been significantly retarded by the combined impact of autarkic, protectionist, trade policies in many developing countries (though a considerable number of these are now being liberalized), and discriminatory trade barriers (tariff quotas and voluntary export restraints, or VERs) raised against their products in developed countries. An important lesson is that continued protectionism has been, and remains, a dampening, and damaging, influence on globalization through trade. Thus, while a good deal of global integration has occurred through trade, it is uneven and sustained by political will, as has been manifested in successive rounds of multilateral and regional trade liberalization.

There is far less globalization in respect of *labour movement.* Despite fear in the West about millions of actual or potential immigrants, and the creation of new ethnic minorities in western Europe, it cannot seriously be claimed that contemporary globalization has much to do with labour movements. At most, 2 per cent of the world's population live outside their country of origin (Castles and Miller, 1993). And the total global flow of migrants (estimated at 25–30 million in the 1980s, many of them temporary refugees) was 0.5 per cent of the world's population. Even in the US, arguably the most open of the important host countries, the annual inflows – around 600,000 – are only half the levels reached in the

Figure 1.3: United States immigration by continent, 1820–1989

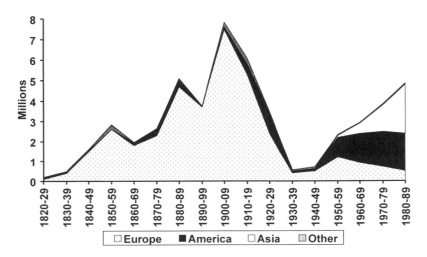

Source: Statistical Abstract of the United States.

period 1900–20 and, as a proportion of the host country population, immigration is much lower now than throughout the period from 1830 to 1920 (Figure 1.3).

The only concerted attempt to create 'national treatment' for migrant workers has been within the EU single market. But realization of free movement has been very slow despite cross-border rights to welfare benefits, freedom from controls, some mutual recognition of qualifications and substantial wage differentials. In the GATT, attempts to create even a minimal degree of access to overseas workers, as service providers, have foundered. Thus, whatever globalization may be it has little, or nothing, to do with creating a global market for labour.

Economic globalization centres on capital movements. Much of the literature on globalization is inspired by the role of multinational companies and *foreign direct investment* (Julius,1990, Turner,1991). From the beginning of the 1980s, FDI flows have grown much faster than world output, or trade, or domestic fixed investment (Figure 1.4). The upshot is that the role of multinational companies – put at 40,000 parent firms with 250,000 foreign affiliates and overseas assets valued at $2.6 trillion (1995) – is, on some measures, greater than that of conventional arm's length trade in integrating the world economy. Global sales of foreign

7

Figure 1.4: FDI flows, 1980–95

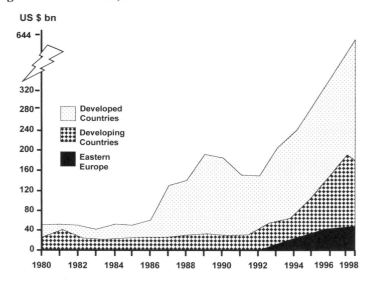

Source: UNCTAD, *World Investment Report*, various years.

affiliates – an estimated $5.2 trillion in 1992 – were substantially greater than global arm's length trade ($3 trillion). Another $2 bn of sales were generated by enterprises linked by other forms of transnational association than FDI: licensing and franchising or sub-contracting.

Does this growth amount to a qualitatively different, denationalized, system of production and exchange, as some of the more ebullient observers have claimed? There are grounds for some scepticism. First, the present-day multinational company has its precursors in the merchant houses and banks of medieval Europe, the trading companies of imperial Britain and the – mainly British – mining, manufacturing and other companies which invested, and produced, overseas on a large scale at the end of the nineteenth century (Dunning,1993; Hirst and Thompson, 1996). Attempts to construct the scale of direct investment in 1914 (Jones,1997) suggest that the ratio of FDI stock to trade was comparable to today's. Overall capital flows appear to have been on a proportionately larger scale (relative to GDP) in the pre-1914 period than in the last decade.

Second, the rapid growth in FDI in recent years has yet to achieve real breadth and sustained momentum. The initial burst of FDI in the late 1980s was almost entirely in developed countries (over 80 per cent of the total) and predominantly from five leading developed countries (over two-thirds). In the 1990s, although developing countries began to attract substantial FDI, 80 per cent of it has been in ten countries, led by China. Even in the developed countries, the share of FDI in total fixed investment has flattened out and is now back to the levels of the mid-1980s. In the UK, one of the most open economies, foreign direct investment accounts for barely 10 per cent of domestic fixed investment.

A third claim, that modern FDI is unique in being truly global in its approach to the organization of production, does not fully stand up to critical examination either. While there is undoubtedly a move towards internationally integrated production in some fields – the car industry for example – and there are global markets in some corporate services, most multinational companies still have the majority of their asset base, shareholders and labour force in their countries of origin. The main exceptions are international oil and mining companies, which have to invest at the point of resource extraction, and companies from small European countries with a very limited domestic market. The major global companies – Microsoft, IBM, General Motors, General Electric, Ford, Pepsico and the leading Japanese multinationals – are still heavily dominated by their home country operations, and this is reflected in their top management and their system of corporate governance. In some key functions, such as R&D, the trend may even be in the opposite direction to globalization (Cantwell, 1992) though that is contested (Reich, 1992) and most R&D for companies such as IBM and Microsoft takes place in the US. Some companies which tried to move their headquarters overseas (such as IBM's network system and Nestlé, both to the UK) reversed the decision later.

When full allowance is made for these various qualifications, however, it is clear that both qualitative and quantitative changes are taking place in the world of international business and that there is both a widening and deepening of international integration through the medium of foreign direct investment.

First, the 1990s have seen a genuine geographical broadening of FDI. Julius's work on FDI global companies described comprehensively the way in which the FDI 'explosion' of the 1980s was characterized by investment flows within the 'triad' of the EU, Japan and North America, was market-driven (rather than driven by wage differentials or natural resource availability) and was increasingly characterized by trade in services as well as manufacturers (Julius, 1990). Since then, the flows to non-OECD countries have increased strikingly in absolute terms and as a

9

share of the total. These flows are accounted for mainly by a small number of Asian countries – China, Singapore, Malaysia, Thailand, Indonesia – but increasingly, also, by Latin America (especially Mexico, Chile, Argentina and Brazil) and eastern Europe (notably Hungary). FDI remains largely market-driven but includes significant amounts attracted by low labour costs for exports and the extractive sector, especially energy.

The non-OECD world has also become a substantial supplier of FDI, which has led to Korean and Taiwanese companies (Daewoo, Hyundai, Samsung) becoming internationally well known. Chinese family companies have invested heavily throughout Southeast Asia, and occasionally beyond (the Riady family from Indonesia; Hutchison Whampoa – the Li Ka-Shing family; Gordon Wu's Hopewell Holdings). Chinese state companies, notably CITIC, have become important in overseas investment. The newly privatized Russian oil companies are among the largest in the world. Gazprom is by far the largest gas company in the world, in terms of the value of reserves, and is spreading a network of companies and investment throughout western Europe. The more traditional OPEC state companies have also invested heavily overseas; PDVSA is one of the largest refiners in the US.

Second, scale is less important than it was. The share of the largest 100 companies (by turnover) in the USA has fallen steadily over the last two decades. Hundreds, or thousands, of medium-sized companies are finding it relatively simple to organize multi-country operations with the help of cheap and easy telecommunications, email and fax communications, frequent visits, the widespread use of English as a common language and the adoption of common, recognized technical and quality standards. Arguably, the smaller multinational companies have some advantages over the bigger, high-profile players in terms of speed and flexibility of response; they also do not have to face the same political and negotiation problems.

Third, there has been a growth of major corporate alliances at a global level. There have been major attempts to construct telecom alliances – most recently between BT and AT&T. Even before the recent spate of mergers (Exxon and Mobil, BP and Arco), there were numerous alliances in the oil industry (BP and Mobil in Europe; Shell and Texaco in the US and with Exxon in the North Sea), usually agreed for specific projects or countries. The vehicles industry has produced many others (Rover and Honda, then BMW; Ford and Opal). Alliances can be limited to specific fields such as R&D. Such alliances can avoid the politically and legally difficult issues involved in takeovers and equity swaps while providing specific economies of scale, complementary business interests and spreading risk.

Fourth, although services and manufacturing sectors dominate FDI flows, companies are also seeking to fill the gaps created by the privatization of utilities in many countries. French water companies have invested in the UK water industry and railways. US electricity generators and distributors have moved overseas. The leading new private generators include a multinational, US-based, gas company (Enron) breaking down the traditional industry barriers within the energy sector. In China power stations are being built by an expatriate property developer (Hopewell), and in India by all manner of Indian and non-Indian energy and non-energy companies. The traditional boundary between industry and services is being made largely meaningless in the complex, interconnected world of telecommunications, computers, software, entertainment and TV. In sum, then, globalization reflects, and encourages, a general 'blurring of boundaries', sectoral as well as national.

Finally, the way companies are managed is also responding to the mechanisms of globalization. The traditional model of the multinational company is that it is multi-domestic, with distinct operations in different countries. In some cases a virtue was made of a highly decentralized mode of decision-making which tried to take maximum advantage of local specificities (market understanding; political sensitivities; high-quality local staff). Shell is an example. Globalization has, however, also empowered the corporate centre by making electronic communications and continuous surveillance much easier. And in some cases, corporate centres have largely dissolved to create electronic networks across national and functional boundaries linking business to the Chief Executive or Executive Board: the so-called 'networked corporation'. It has additionally given some companies the confidence to plan their production on a global basis to maximize the gains from transport and other cost savings (Ford), and specialization by function rather than country (research labs by Hewlett Packard, for example).

Information technology and cheap telecommunications create an ambiguous split of costs and benefits from centralization and decentralization and the market for different corporate services is globalized to various degrees. Figure 1.5 tries to indicate impressionistically how these different markets are working. There is in major corporations increasingly a global market for treasury management, reflecting the globalization of financial markets, senior specialist staff (geologists, IT systems

Figure 1.5: Optimum globalization of corporate activities

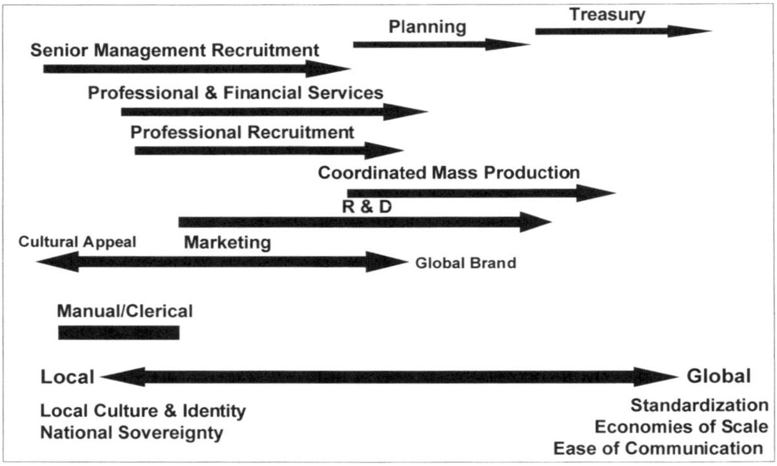

Source: Author (Shell Planning).

engineers) and professional services, and a move towards integrated production systems where feasible, but leaving some activities domestically rooted.

One field in which globalization may begin to approximate both to the truly global – in the sense of globally integrated systems – and to complete economic integration – resulting in globally uniform prices – is *financial markets*. Richard O'Brien has coined the term 'the end of geography' to describe a world in which national regulators no longer hold sway over their regulatory territory; where financial firms increasingly function as globally integrated businesses, not just as multinational companies; where stock markets are open to foreign portfolio investors and no longer monopolize the trading of shares in 'their' national companies; and where companies can avail themselves of a wide variety of services from financial institutions which have easy access to different – geographical and product – markets (O'Brien, 1992).

But, as with other aspects of globalization, it is not immediately clear that we are dealing with something fundamentally different and new. In the Middle Ages, there were multinational banks (the Lombards), cross-border sovereign lending and trade in securitized financial instruments

Figure 1.6: Capital mobility index

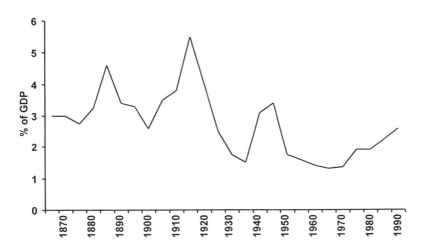

Source: Alan M. Taylor, National Bureau of Economic Research, Washington DC.

such as commercial bills (Dunning, 1993). The boom in international bank lending which characterized the decade before the 1982 debt crisis had many parallels in history; there were waves of large-scale lending to governments, and defaults, throughout the nineteenth century. The more recent growth of international securitized (bond) issues was also paralleled throughout the nineteenth century when major projects – such as the Suez and Panama canals or South American railways – were partly financed through long-term bond issues to international investors. As a consequence of high levels of bank and bond borrowing, external country debt sometimes became higher than would be considered prudent even today. One recent measure of short-term capital mobility suggests capital liberalization has considerably increased flows but to levels well below those before the First World War (Figure 1.6).

One way of testing the integration of international markets is to measure the extent to which there is real interest parity between financial assets in different currencies. A very high degree of interest rate equalization was achieved before the First World War, and the current international financial integration is arguably less advanced than at that time (Turner, 1991). Analysis of the degree of capital market integration based

13

on different measures of transnational securities trading and ownership suggests that markets were more integrated before 1914 than they are now (Zevin, 1992) – indeed the process was well advanced by the middle of the eighteenth century. Analysis of correlations between domestic savings and investment suggests that although there is international transmission of savings from savings-rich, mainly Asian, countries to the savings-'poor' US, the overall separation between the two is not large – as one would expect of an internationally integrated system – and is not obviously growing (Hirst and Thompson, 1996). Indeed the financial crisis in 1998 originated in unsustainable capital flows into, not out of, savings-rich economies such as South Korea.

Moreover, while there has been much interest in portfolio diversification into new markets by asset managers, the actual diversification is very limited, especially in the US and France (limited though it has been, there was enough to cause a stampede from perceived high-risk markets in 1998). Moreover, there are still major access barriers to foreign investors and to foreign banking and fund management institutions in many countries, even within the single market of the EU (Steil, 1998). The upshot is that even in the most outward-looking of societies such as the UK and the Netherlands only 15–20% of household financial assets are held in overseas bonds and equities; just over 10 per cent in the US; and under 5 per cent in France, Japan, Italy and Spain.

While global financial integration is far from having reached 'the end of geography', there is a considerable integration dynamic. In practice there are several specific ways in which the globalization of financial markets is having profound implications for the way in which business is transacted and the way governments function. First, the volume of trading in different currencies now far exceeds the volume of trades needed for transaction purposes and is overwhelmingly concerned with arbitrage and hedging activities. According to the Bank of International Settlements, the London foreign exchange markets' daily turnover in April 1998 was around $640 bn, New York's $350 bn and Tokyo's $150 bn, with increases since 1992 of respectively 37 per cent and 43 per cent for London and New York. These figures so far exceed official reserves that in practice governments no longer have any mechanism for 'managing' their exchange rates other than by maintaining market confidence and through interest rates. Second, governments and corporate borrowers are now subject to the disciplines of international bond markets which, with the mediation of rating agencies, set in effect a global price for country and corporate risk and inflation expectations. Third, and most topically, the freeing up of capital flows consequent upon the removal of exchange controls has liberated large volumes of short-term capital movements which can have an enormous impact especially in small markets. Unlike the mainly long-term portfolio flows of the nineteenth century, today's flows are increasingly highly leveraged. Global hedge fund resources deployed in emerging markets amount to an estimated $400 bn, excluding leverage of five or six times investors' funds. A relatively modest portfolio adjustment in response to changes on perceived risk – in the form of margin calls by banks lending to the funds – can have an enormous impact on narrow markets (even before the recent crash, South Korea, Thailand and Indonesia had combined equity market capitalization of well under $400 bn).

To summarize, financial market integration may not be fundamentally different, conceptually, from what has occurred in the past. Overall, capital mobility may be less today than in the nineteenth century. But new technology means that the speed of transmission of large flows of finance is enormously greater; and higher speeds bring a larger capacity for sudden shocks and for the rapid spread of panic: the concerns which lay at the heart of the 1998 crisis.

The driving forces: the two revolutions

It is as easy to minimize as to exaggerate the phenomenon of globalization, as of other revolutionary changes. It would have been easy for a visitor to France after 1789 to point to the unchanging rhythms of rural life and the drudgery of daily existence and ask: 'what revolution?' It would, today, be easy to wander around much of the former Soviet Union – where the physical drabness of Soviet urban architecture, collective farms, busts of Lenin and factories run by former communist apparatchiks still abound – and conclude that nothing much has happened.

With all the necessary qualifications to the hyperbole about globalization, something important is happening: two overlapping trends of considerable momentum. One is technological, the speeding up of communications. Many communications improvements have been taking place over the last century, but the contemporary speed of change, the enlargement of capacity for information (and capital) transmission and the proliferation of communications media have not been experienced before.

The other is a change in the policy environment: a 'liberalization revolution', a freeing up of markets and reduction in the role of government in terms of ownership and control over production of goods and services.

15

These two changes are related. Traditional, centralized state structures have been unable to manage, or withstand, the corrosive effects of information technology. Improved communications reduce effective distance for the transmission of information and thus the degree of monopoly control which nation-state governments can exercise even over such sensitive expressions of national identity as culture and use of language. Simultaneously, the 'liberalization revolution' challenges the legitimacy of many of the activities nation-state governments have performed in the 'modern' (post-1914) world: running nationalized industries; trade, exchange and price controls, and monopoly control over infrastructure and public services (Strange, 1996).

These two forces reinforce each other in different ways in different sectors, which means that the impact of globalization is uneven. In some sectors there has been little liberalization and challenge to the state's protective role, and information technology has been a weak influence. These include agriculture, for example (though pressures to cut government support and the new advances in biotechnology could well have major implications in future, which is why the genetically modified foods debate is not just about science and the environment but also about trade policy). Activities such as mining or chemicals manufacturing were already subject to reasonably free trade and competitive private enterprise in many countries and are, if anything, moving towards greater (environmental) regulation. The energy sector – notably oil – was in some respects already 'globalized' decades ago, though other segments, especially gas, are now seeing the full impact of deregulation and international exchange (through pipelines and liquefied natural gas carriers). Some manufacturing sectors – car production and textiles, for example – have seen a major transformation in technological possibilities and production organization on a global basis but the policy regime, particularly trade policy, has changed little.

There are, however, other sectors where policy reform and rapid technological change are powerfully reinforcing each other. Here the dilemmas posed by 'globalization' are most acute and the uncertainties greatest. These are the sectors we shall draw upon for many of our examples. All are concerned with communications in the widest sense.

The telecommunications industry is seeing the deregulation and/or privatization of telecoms utilities almost everywhere (Figure 1.7); the rapid introduction of new technologies including competing systems (wire and wireless); integration with other industries (multimedia); the

Figure 1.7: Privatization and deregulation in basic telecoms services

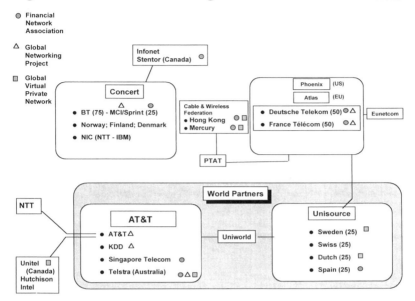

Source: Cable and Distler, 1995.

creation of corporate global alliances; global (and regional) standard-setting; and attempts to create new global and regional rules for market access and competition (Cable and Distler, 1995).

Financial services have already experienced major changes: a deregulation 'big bang' in some major countries; a transformation of the industry's technology with efficient, computerized clearing and settlement systems, and enormous increases in the speed and quantity of financial flows; intense competition among leading global financial companies; and the agreement of global and regional rules for market access, competition, regulation for systemic risk and standards. Indeed the recent global financial crisis has exposed rather brutally the extent to which technology and market liberalization have run ahead of rules and systems of governance.

Data transmission and information networks have already seen, largely outside the reach of governments, the creation of global networks (the Internet), and widely recognized global standards (MS DOS) and companies which facilitate information transmission using them. With digital technology, it is no longer meaningful or useful to distinguish telecommunications and computer networking; the new TV decoders will enable users to access the Internet through the same piece of equipment used to watch satellite television. So far, discussion of the competition and market access issues at a global level has scarcely begun.

Entertainment and media industries Since the means of transmission (telecommunications and information networks) cannot in practice be separated from their content, there is considerable overlap with the 'industries' supplying information, news and entertainment. Here, powerful global technological drivers (cable and satellite TV; CD-ROM) have been colliding with national systems of regulation designed to control quality, cultural values and access to offensive material. Global companies are also emerging and there are growing pressures to create regional and global rules – so far embryonic – related to market access for media suppliers, protection of intellectual property and standards governing content.

Airlines, too, have seen a traditional system of (mostly) national monopolies rapidly giving way to deregulation and privatization. Technological advance has radically changed the product (the speed and size of aircraft) and inputs (booking systems). In a parallel with telecommunications, attempts are being made to create principles for competition and market access as between operators, which are increasingly private and global, and to adapt regulation (safety, flight lanes and air traffic control) accordingly.

All of these sectors – several of which now overlap – pose immensely tricky problems of balancing competition against regulatory controls and of striking the best balance between national, regional and global regimes as they relate to standard-setting, network management, public safety, systemic risk and other sources of externalities. Before dealing with these in detail in the context of the evolving system of global governance, let us consider how far the globalization process is permanent and durable.

No turning back

Views of the future are inevitably coloured by interpretations of the present. Crudely caricatured, these range from the uncompromising belief that we now live in a borderless world from which there is no retreat to the sceptical view that nothing has really changed.

The sceptics are important for reminding us, first, of historical precedents for the reversal of what seemed at the time to be an inexorable trend towards greater economic integration. The unravelling of the nineteenth-century system of free trade and capital flows, and fixed exchange rates, in the face of war, depression and economic nationalism is a salutary tale and, although conditions are now very different, it is not impossible that diminishing global demand and a reversion to protectionist trade policies could lead to a downward spiral of contracting trade as occurred after 1929 (Figure 1.8).

The sceptics also remind us that globalization is not driven by some *deus ex machina*. The commitment to economic policy liberalization and open economies is ultimately subject to the politics of major countries. There has been in recent years a broad acceptance that – in Margaret Thatcher's words – 'There Is No Alternative'. The simplicity of political

Figure 1.8: The contracting spiral of world trade, January 1929–March 1933

Total imports of 75 countries (billions of US gold dollars)

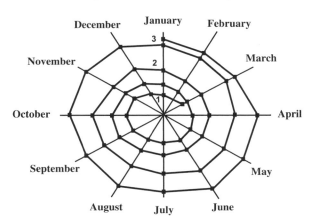

Source: Kindleberger, 1973.

Figure 1.9: Progress in liberalization

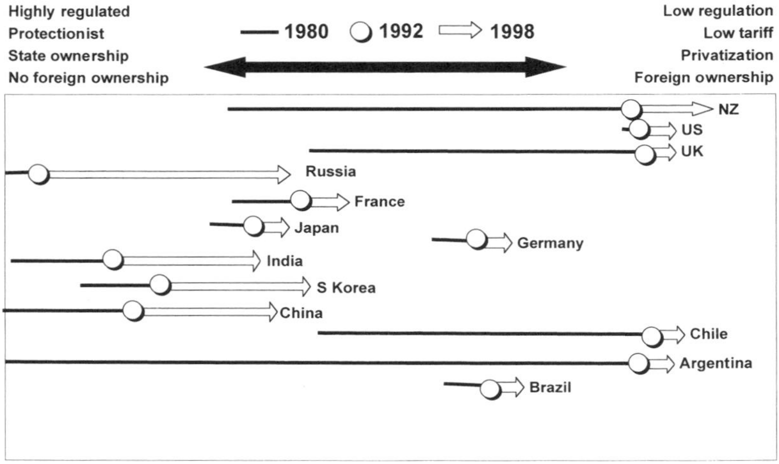

Source: Author (Shell Planning).

slogans is, however, obscured by the detail of what happens at country or sector level in the many policy spheres covered by the umbrella concept of 'liberalization': removal of barriers to trade, foreign investment and exchange controls; freeing of product and factor markets; rules-based systems of regulation; policy regimes favouring financial stability.

First, Figure 1.9, in a very rough and ready way, gives an impressionistic snapshot of what is happening globally. Almost all major countries are moving in the direction of policy liberalization. East Asian countries – notably South Korea and Japan, which long argued that their successful model vindicated a measure of protectionism – are being forced, by crisis, to reform. The countries of western Europe which long argued that they also had a distinctive approach are preparing for the more intense market competition that follows the creation of a single market and, now, of a single currency. France has within the last decade overturned a long mercantilist tradition by accepting trade liberalization under the WTO and now actively welcomes foreign investment. There has been no discernible retreat from the commitment to policy liberalization across Latin America – where Brazil has been belatedly accepting reforms – or in eastern Europe. The main doubts centre on three major countries which have only recently and tentatively emerged from near-autarky:

India (though the nationalist BJP government has already retreated on its plans to reverse the liberalization of foreign investment rules and import controls); China (which is pressing ahead with radical plans to expose its state enterprises to commercial disciplines but has also retreated on various measures – for example, the opening up of telecoms to foreign investment or import liberalization); and Russia where the radical, if precarious, liberalization of the post-Soviet period could still be reversed.

Second, where economically illiberal policies are being introduced or contemplated, it is usually for specific reasons rather than as part of a fundamental change in economic philosophy. There is little sign of trade protectionism re-emerging as a major force (though there are influential advocates in the US). Moves to liberalize trade in financial services and telecommunications, globally, have been belatedly agreed. There are few, if any, countries seeking to raise barriers, let alone to expropriate direct foreign investors (though even the most open economies still have numerous loopholes favouring domestic companies). The North Korean 'model' has few, if any, advocates.

One area of retreat is freedom from controls of short-term capital flows. Restrictions in Malaysia in particular may herald a new period of scepticism about the value of removing exchange controls, at least in emerging markets. To date, however, controls have been introduced for temporary and economically plausible reasons, to permit domestic interest rate cuts (Malaysia) or in support of a broader commitment to market liberalization (Chile) by reducing financial market volatility. There is, moreover, serious questioning of whether free short-term capital flows are inevitable or desirable (Wolf, 1998) – of which more below.

There are good reasons for believing that a major policy reversal is highly unlikely, though not impossible. First, technology is a very powerful driving force in its own right. Cross-border information flows will increase, whatever the mood of policy-makers. Because of electronically driven commerce, there is growing trade over the Internet. The same medium facilitates the exchange of ideas and creativity from design to entertainment. The so-called 'weightless economy' (Quah, 1996) is easily internationalized since the biggest natural impediment to trade is bulk.

Second, systems of international governance – rules and institutions – are much more developed and robust than those which evolved in the 1930s. We shall look at these in more detail below.

Third, despite the sense of drama surrounding the crisis in 1998, it does not yet compare with the inter-war period. It is estimated that there was a fall of 6 per cent in GDP in Korea and 20 per cent in Indonesia, and

Table 1.1 Great economic disasters of the twentieth century

Country	% fall, peak to trough	Years to recover to pre-disaster levels
US (and Canada)	30	1929–39 (10)
UK	19	1918–35 (17)
France	50	1929–49 (20)
Italy	44	1940–49 (9)
Germany	58	1944–53 (9)
Japan	52	1943–53 (10)
Netherlands	50	1939–47 (8)
Austria	38	1913–28 (12)
	25	1929–39 (10)
	60	1941–53 (12)
Soviet Union	60+ (?)	1989–? (?)

Source: Table based on Maddison, 1995.

world growth of 2 per cent (half the previous year's). Recovery was already apparent in several of the Asian countries in 1999. By contrast in the Great Depression GDP in the US fell 30 per cent and took ten years to recover to the same output level; the UK GDP fell 25 per cent and took 18 years to recover (Table 1.1). The 1998 crisis was minor by comparison but could be the harbinger of trouble to come.

Is globalization desirable?

Whether or not deeper global economic integration is irresistible depends in large measure on whether it is broadly felt to be desirable. The process of market liberalization which has helped to drive globalization is, at root, political and depends on popular support or, at least, acceptance.

Benefits

Behind globalization lies considerably more than a hope and a prayer and a burst of new technology: a solid edifice of economic theory and the practical lessons of economic history. Arguments for free trade have been advanced for 2,500 years and have held the intellectual high ground for most of the last two centuries (Irwin, 1996).

A contemporary statement of the economic benefits of globalization would draw first on various strands of theory: traditional (Ricardian) trade theory illustrating the efficiency gains from specialization between countries with different resource endowments; the benefits of economies of scale on an international level (first clearly described by Adam Smith); the stimulus to efficiency from increased competition (Leibenstein, 1966); the benefits of trade creation, scale and competition within regional groups (Viner, 1950, Balassa, 1961); and the costs of protection in the form of rent-seeking behaviour (Bhagwati, 1998; Corden, 1974). To these would be added the arguments for achieving benefits of specialization, scale and competition through direct investment flows as well as trade and the spread of technology and 'best practice' through multinational companies (Grossman and Helpman, 1991; Dunning, 1993). The adoption of these arguments by UNCTAD has been an important change in the intellectual climate. A more contemporary and controversial case has been made for globally free capital markets on grounds of efficiency and competition (Eichengreen, Mussa et al., 1998). All of this work supports the notion that there is potential benefit from open rather than closed economies.

A crucially important additional strand of support has come from contemporary welfare economics, deriving from the theory of the second best which is specifically directed to the problems faced by activist modern governments anxious to deal with environmental failures, inequality and other social ills. This shows that these objectives will invariably be achieved more efficiently by forms of government intervention that do not discriminate against foreigners, such as on imports, inward investment or immigrants (Corden, 1974).

The structure of supporting theory would mean little if it were not reflected in economic reality. The enduring support (with, of course, many specific exceptions) for liberal economic policies and international integration derives credibility from historical, and contemporary, experience of rapid economic growth associated with rapid trade growth (Boltho, 1996; Maddison, 1995); the negative experiences of periods of protectionism and of 'rent-seeking' behaviour (Bhagwati, 1982); the contrast between export-led development in East Asia and southern Europe and inward-looking development in Latin America (Krugman, 1994a; Little, Skitovsky and Scott, 1990); the failure and pathological excesses of autarky in North Korea, Cambodia, or Burma; and the wider failure of the socialist system of the USSR and COMECON, largely isolated from international capitalism.

A further factor is the ability of countries to demonstrate the advantages of virtually complete economic openness, embracing globalization, while achieving a high level of political commitment to equality and income distribution, universal services, environmental protection and workers' rights (Netherlands, Sweden, Denmark, Ireland, Canada and Australia). Some of the more successful emerging economies (Taiwan and South Korea) have also managed to reconcile growth with low levels of inequality.

The critics

Globalization has its critics, and they are important in setting the terms of the political debate, discussed further in Chapter 2. There are essentially three strands which can be separated out. The first, and most fundamental, is an extension of the Marxist-Leninist critique of capitalism to the world economy: the idea that international economic integration is an inherent part of a process of exploitation of labour and of weak commodity-producing countries. The arguments have been updated (Emmanuel, 1972; Barratt Brown, 1974) mostly in the context of the post-colonial debate on development and were very influential in the 1960s in encouraging ideas of 'de-linkage' and 'self-reliance', free from 'dependency' on Western-dominated international capitalism (Samir Amin, 1993). They still provide a conscious, or unconscious, underpinning for a number of contemporary arguments despite the failure of alternative models of development based on Marxist ideology, or 'self-reliance'.

A second strand is less radical and operates within an essentially neo-classical framework: identifying specific instances where maldistribution of the gains from trade (or investment) might justify a major departure from liberal policy in respect of trade or investment.

There is the classic 'terms of trade' argument advanced by Prebisch (1959) and others – which was highly influential in the 1950s and 1960s – to justify a conscious strategy to diversify from commodity exporting to manufactures, protected from international competition. It is certainly possible to demonstrate theoretically, and with examples, that commodity-based export growth can be immiserizing if all the benefits of export expansion are all passed on to importers in lower prices (Bhagwati, 1958). And there has been in practice a long-term trend of decline in barter terms of trade for primary commodities. But one lesson from experience has been that manufactured products are a much better route to diversification than highly protected import substitutes which in Latin America and India proved, after an initial burst of industrial growth, to be inefficient, unsustainable in terms of external payments and a cause of widening inequality (Little, Skitovsky and Scott, 1990). Arguments for protectionism based on protected industrialization now enjoy little credibility, but they have a lingering influence in countries such as India.

A different argument is that advanced countries relatively well endowed with capital rather than labour, when trading with labour-abundant, low-wage countries will tend (under some rather restrictive assumptions) to see wages decline relative to other income sources (Stolper and Samuelson, 1941). This proposition is used to argue that rich countries may have to protect themselves against 'cheap' labour to prevent a decline in the real wages (and working conditions) of their industrial workers, particularly the unskilled. The arguments have been advanced in the political arena with varying degrees of crudity and the populist potential has been exploited recently, especially in the US (by Ross Perot) and less successfully in Europe (by the late Sir James Goldsmith). Some impetus has been given to the debate by serious research suggesting that unskilled wages may not have grown as fast as GDP in some rich countries – notably the US – because of import competition (and immigration) (Wood, 1994). Other empirical studies dispute the facts or, while accepting some degree of downward pressure on unskilled wages from international trade competition and immigration, argue that these are relatively minor compared with the impact of technology or the wider policy environment (Lawrence and Slaughter, 1993; Baldwin, 1988; Learner, 1996; Slaughter and Swagel, 1997). And most economists, even if disagreeing on the facts, would argue that trade protectionism (or curbs on direct investment) is a very poor, and unsustainable, way to improve wages and conditions of industrial-sector workers.

One recent addition to the set of well-worn arguments has come from so-called 'strategic trade theory' which has created a new set of justifications for national governments to interpose themselves between the world economy and domestic business (Brander and Spencer, 1985; Laussel, Montet and Feissole, 1988). In some respects, these arguments update very old 'infant industry' arguments for temporary protection based on possible externalities or other arguments for consciously turning the terms of trade against other counties (the 'optimum tariff'). But they go further to incorporate game theory to describe the interactions between small numbers of large companies and governments in such industries as aerospace, satellite communications, basic telecommunications and computer software. Much of the empirical work does not suggest that 'strategic' intervention by governments has the positive effects claimed for it (Venables and Smith, 1990; Dixit, 1987; Krugman, 1986) and, in any event, few of the proponents of 'strategic' intervention are suggesting a whole-scale withdrawal from international economic integration as opposed to attempts to intervene in some special cases.

In addition to these well-established academic debates there is emerging a third strand: what could be called 'the new protectionism'. What is striking in the literature about some of the 'new protectionism' is that it is not, in fact, very new and draws extensively on dependency theory and the 'economics of imperialism' (Lang and Hines, 1993; Barratt Brown, 1974). Much of it, also, could not be dignified by calling it economic argument since it repudiates many of the most fundamental sources of economic advance and rising living standards (specialization; economies of scale) in favour of 'self-reliant' communities and countries.

But some of the more sophisticated texts (Daly and Goodland, 1992) introduce some genuinely challenging ideas. The most important concerns the pervasive nature of environmental crisis: the irrevocable loss of environmental assets such as tropical forests or fish stocks and the impact of pollution on such traditional 'sinks' as the atmosphere, the ozone layer and the oceans. The problem with this approach is that even if the pessimistic analysis of global environmental trends is valid (and this is vigorously disputed), there is no logical link between a concern for the environment and protectionist approaches to trade and investment. First, there is now a well-developed field of environmental economics demonstrating that environmental externalities should be dealt with by applying the 'polluter pays principle' through taxation or regulatory instruments; in no way does it justify discriminating against imports over domestic production or against foreign investment over domestic capitalists (Cairncross, 1991). Second, there is an underlying trend – intensified by the competitive pressures of globalization – towards dematerialization and more efficient resource use (one consequence of which is weakening commodity prices). Third, 'self-reliance' has a bad history. The world's most serious examples of environmental degradation and wasteful resource use are in the former USSR and Northern China which developed without the discipline of markets or access to good environmental practice through foreign investment and trade. Fourth, the link between extreme poverty and environmental stress is well established. 'Self-reliant' subsistence agriculture and nomadic practices can be immensely destructive of the natural environment in conditions of rising population; far more than multinational agribusinesses. More serious treatment of environmental sustainability has stressed the importance of international economic integration (Brundtland, 1987).

The one specific concern of environmentalists is that trade, as such, generates environmental pollution through cross-border transport. The point is valid as far as it goes but is trivial in relation to the sum of environmental externalities and could be addressed by taxing all road and air freight traffic on the 'polluter pays principle', not by stopping trade.

There are some unifying themes in the old and the new criticisms of globalization which represent entirely valid concerns even if they lead to the wrong conclusions. One is that globalization provides for cross-border capital, rather than labour, mobility and is therefore more likely to improve returns to capital rather than labour. Modern manifestations of globalization centre on the rapid growth of foreign direct investment and short-term capital flows rather than trade in goods or – even more – labour movements. The appropriate answer to this asymmetry, however, is not to retreat into national or regional autarky but to open markets to labour-intensive products and services (removing current biases against these items in tariff and other protective structures in rich countries) and to seek to extend liberalizing trade rules to labour-only services (blocked by rich countries at present).

The other worry is that the gap between rich and poor countries is widening. Few reports on the state of the world fail to point out that the distribution of income internationally is massively skewed though there is an enormous range of estimates depending largely upon whether income per capita is measured in nominal prices and exchange rates or in purchasing power equivalents, the latter being less extreme. Maddison's work on long-term economic trends (1995) shows that the degree of divergence between 'rich' and 'poor' has grown steadily in a century and a half of modernization and growing integration, albeit in the context of generally rising absolute standards. In 1820 the per capita incomes in pre-colonial Africa at present prices were around $450, $625 in China, and $1,135 in pre-industrial Japan. These figures are not enormously lower than those of the world's richest country at that time, Britain – with around $1,750 – or the European average of around $1,225. While African and Indian incomes have roughly doubled in over a century and a half to $840 and $1,350 respectively, those of western Europe have multiplied 14 times and Japan 17 times. The gap between the richest and poorest country in Maddison's sample of 56 countries has widened from a ratio of 1:3 to 1:72 (that is, between the US and Ethiopia). The period of postwar growth has widened disparities considerably overall but has also reduced disparities between the rich and those countries that are rapidly catching up (in East and Southeast Asia, and in southern Europe) while creating a new class of under-performers in Latin America and eastern Europe. The 1980s and 1990s have produced a new crop of catch-up candidates including, notably, China (and, more tentatively, the countries of South Asia and Egypt).

But is globalization part of the problem or part of the solution? Disparities are undoubtedly much more evident as a result of improved communications. Extreme wealth and world poverty are graphically brought into everyone's living room where they result in a mixture of envy, resentment, admiration, self-satisfaction, guilt and indifference. Liberalization and globalization may have also undermined highly egalitarian domestic policies, and the values associated with them. This is because of wider opportunities for successful entrepreneurs, stars, mobile firms and individuals and the highly educated and also because highly progressive tax structures are not easily enforcible, since rich people and capital are mobile and can avoid high rates.

But it is difficult to sustain seriously the view that global economic integration is inexorably creating growing inequality. Those countries in southern Europe and East Asia which have sought most actively to develop through international economic integration have seen their income levels converge with those of the rich world. The largest concentration of global poverty is in India and China, both of which, while now growing rapidly under the stimulus of economic reforms, opted for several decades to pursue isolationist economic policies. The poorest countries, in Africa, have large numbers of subsistence farmers and have become marginalized from global economic integration because poor infrastructure and governance, and political instability, have prevented much meaningful development taking place at all. The argument of anti-globalization critics that Africa has been impoverished by its – limited amount of – cash-crop farming or multinational companies is a travesty of the truth: the former has in fact made a modest contribution to rural incomes and generally improved farming practices; most of the latter have reduced their exposure to Africa.

Extent, timing and sequence

The serious practical debates about globalization are not in fact concerned with the extremes of total integration or total isolation. Even those countries with very liberal trade and investment policies retain immigration controls. With a few pathological extremes such as Pol Pot's Cambodia, Kim Il Sung's North Korea or Enver Hoxha's Albania there have been few examples, and few advocates, of extreme autarky. In practice the arguments are about the speed and extent of liberalization – opening up the global economy: the sequencing and the conditions required to make liberalization successful. The opening up of 'transitional' – former planned – economies has given focus to this debate.

Experience is showing that there are big differences in adjustment problems as between small European countries such as Estonia and Slovenia and small states in Central Asia such as Tajikistan and Kyrgyzstan; large, mainly agricultural, states such as China or India and big industrial countries such as Russia and Ukraine; countries such as Poland and Hungary with prolonged experience of functioning markets and exposure to Western economies and those such as Belarus or Mongolia with virtually none at all.

There are no simple, coin-in-the-slot answers to the question of how, and how rapidly, countries with economies shaped by decades of 'planning' and 'self-reliance' should be exposed to globalization. There are cases where liberalization is premature or inappropriate. Lifting import barriers may not improve resource allocation if price signals are greatly distorted to start with and there is no mechanism for pointing resources in the direction of comparative advantage. Opening an economy to an influx of foreign direct investment may reduce welfare if the investment goes into activities heavily protected by import restrictions (Little, Skitovsky and Scott, 1990; Cable and Persaud, 1987) or into a monopoly (Hymer, 1967) although some analysis suggests that it is very unlikely that direct foreign investment will actually reduce welfare (Johnson, 1974).

The most serious and widely supported criticism of premature liberalization relates to controls over short-term capital flows. The issue of capital controls is discussed in more detail in Chapter 4 but a consensus is emerging that free capital movements can be destabilizing through their effect on exchange rates and on an underdeveloped, badly supervised and inefficient banking system (Wolf, 1998).

The issue, then, is how closed and highly regulated economies should approach the issue of globalization. Some conclusions are emerging among economic policy-makers:

• First, despite the frequent assumption that liberalization of external transactions should proceed more slowly than for internal markets – to lessen the domestic adjustment costs – there is powerful evidence, especially in Poland, Estonia and Bulgaria, or in Chile and Argentina – that early external liberalization, in parallel with domestic liberalization and stabilization, yields considerable benefits. This applies especially to free trade as a stimulus to enterprise reform, to exports and generally to making markets more competitive. Trade protection, by contrast, is likely to breed inefficiency (Åslund, 1994; Sachs and Warner, 1995).

- Second, the belief that liberalization is most effective when pursued gradually derives largely from China (and to a lesser degree Vietnam) where a slow process of liberalization, not just of trade but of most controls – 'feeling the stones to cross the river', in Deng's words – has been associated with extraordinary growth performance. But there are significant costs from remaining export and import restrictions and there is a mounting awareness, not least in China, that gradual liberalization has inhibited serious reforms of state enterprises (Lardy, 1994; Wall, 1996). The contrast between Poland (and the former Czechoslovakia) – which liberalized trade and current-account exchange transactions in one 'big bang' – and Hungary and Romania suggests greater success for the former.
- There is an established process for the phasing and design of trade liberalization – the 'tariffication' of quotas to create a simplified tariff structure, leading by degrees to a low uniform tariff – which is now being implemented even in the most protectionist of countries, including India (Dean, Desai and Reidel, 1994).
- A much more contentious issue has been the speed of capital convertibility – the lifting of controls on capital inflows and outflows. It has been argued that while direct investment is a stable and reliable way to finance development by linking capital inflows to transfers of good practice and technology, short-term capital flows are more volatile and more likely to be used for consumption. The basis of this distinction has, however, been questioned (Dooley, 1995). And there are arguments for capital liberalization in introducing competition and better practice within the financial sector of emerging markets, quite apart from the wider global arguments. But one clear lesson is that rapid liberalization of capital flows in countries with weak systems of regulation and government intervention in credit allocation can precipitate banking crises and, in the absence of policies leading to macroeconomic stability, can aggravate instability. It is clear, with hindsight, that before capital movements are fully liberalized there has to be a liberalized financial system underpinned by regulation and supervision.

Thus, the answer to the question 'is globalization beneficial?' is that in general it is. But at the level of industrial countries it depends on the specifics of sequencing and timing and on the quality of domestic policies.

Chapter 2

The politics of globalization

National politics in a global economy

Economics may be increasingly global. Politics is still national. No one seriously pretends that bodies such as the European Parliament – let alone the Council of Europe or the Inter-Parliamentary Union – have serious political power in their own right. Where there is international cooperation – in the IMF, the UN, the World Trade Organization, the European Union – it occurs through the mediation of national ministers. The legitimacy of politicians resides essentially in their domestic electorates.

New, truly global organizations of a political character are, however, springing up. Bodies such as Amnesty International have a great deal of influence in setting standards of behaviour for governments and achieving greater political transparency. Their role is analogous to the role of Moody's and Standard and Poor in global bond markets; they are, in effect, political rating agencies. Their influence can be particularly significant in highlighting the deficiencies of governments without any domestic political legitimacy. But where politics is grounded in democratic choice – be it in the US or India, western Europe or almost all of Latin America – politicians are ultimately accountable to domestic constituencies.

There is a growing tension between deepening economic integration and the virtual absence of meaningful political integration. The sense of a 'democratic deficit' is most acute where economic integration is deepest – as in Europe – but is becoming a more serious problem everywhere. The legitimacy of the IMF and the World Trade Organization is being questioned. The grassroots campaign against the OECD Multilateral Investment Agreement – though characterized by much disinformation and confusion – may be a harbinger of what is to come (Henderson, 1999).

31

This chapter seeks to deal with the interaction between politics and globalization by looking first at how national politics is being affected by the loss of traditional areas of national sovereignty, by distributional effects and by a changing sense of national security.

Does globalization threaten the nation-state?

The two sets of changes described above have together provided the impetus behind globalization: technological change, which reduces effective geographical distance, and liberalization of economic policy. Both seem to undermine some of the traditional roles of government: control over flows of information and, perhaps, the definition of cultural values; some aspects of independent national economic management; and the capacity significantly to shift the distribution of income and wealth. In fact, the influence of globalization on the function of nation-states is complex, involving a balance of different forces and different impacts in different policy domains (see Box 2.1).

To start with *communications systems*, globalization seems, at first sight, to undermine some important traditional national, and usually nationalized, monopolies – telephone, TV, radio. International telephone (and fax) traffic is now largely instantaneous, cheap (relative to other goods and services), simple for individuals to access and difficult for governments to block. The Internet provides a genuinely global system of communication and information. Satellite and cable TV and VHF radio

---

Box 2.1: What nation-states can and cannot do

Mainly under national control	*Global forces dominate*
Migration of poor	Migration of rich and educated
Education	News; entertainment
Politics	Political ideas
Public expenditure/tax mix	Top tax rates. Bond markets
Monetary policy (outside monetary union)	Forex markets
Infrastructure	Trade policy rules

have created a cornucopia of choice in news and entertainment. These changes are not merely weakening the power of governments to control what people see and hear but also people's sense of national identity, since media content can be both global (CNN, Hollywood or 'Bollywood' films, Internet conferences) and very local or tribal (ethnic-language broadcasting and television). These changes are profound but – equally – should not be exaggerated. Governments can control the production and use of necessary hardware – satellite dishes, modems, fax machines – as China is doing. They can control the issue of licences and/or bandwidth allocations for radio, wireless telephones and TV stations. Encryption technology is being developed to safeguard national secrets, as well as private property rights, on computer-based networks. Surveillance of telephone use is already feasible and is being extended to computer networks in the US. Legal control over content – i.e. censorship – is currently being extended via US telecommunications legislation to the Internet and the means exist to enforce censorship through the blocking of specific radio and TV wavebands. Where physical controls are difficult or not feasible, or where the authorities lack the skill to operate them, it is possible to use cultural mobilization against alien and offensive material, as is occurring with Muslim, Christian and Hindu fundamentalists. It would be rash to assume that modern global communications systems will weaken, let alone disable, nation-state governments in the long term.

There is similar ambiguity in relation to *economics* and the supposed loss of national control over economic management. There are several concerns here. The first is that 'global markets' – in particular the $1 trillion (daily turnover) foreign-exchange market – undermine the capacity of governments to set independent national policy objectives, for inflation or unemployment, say. The second is that the high international mobility of some factors of production – long-term as well as short-term capital; highly skilled and professionally qualified workers and managers – greatly circumscribes the ability of governments to influence events through loss of control over industrial location and the income and profits tax base, and through a weakened capacity to impose employment, environmental and other standards. A third concern is that with growing interdependence through trade or capital flows there is a greater vulnerability to external spillovers in the form of shocks or overseas policy changes with adverse domestic effects.

Important though these trends are, there is a tendency to exaggerate the impact of globalization. Many of the constraints on national freedom

33

of action are self-imposed. Governments which choose to operate within a fixed exchange-rate regime – as in the EMU, or using an exchange peg as in Argentina – accept the loss of one of the tools of economic policy management, the nominal exchange rate, as did countries on the nineteenth-century Gold Standard. Those national governments that choose monetary independence are no less able to do so than in earlier times, though the expression of this independence may simply involve the right to choose a higher rate of inflation. Zaire, Serbia, Venezuela and Nigeria have all demonstrated an impressive ability to sustain, independently and for prolonged periods, high inflation and monetary incontinence and others have long survived suppressing the symptoms (North Korea, Cuba). Electronically mediated foreign-exchange and capital markets can signal rapidly and massively any inconsistencies in policy in an open economy but do not, of themselves, eliminate the sovereign right of states to manage, or mismanage, themselves. The debate over EMU is so fierce in the UK precisely because monetary independence is real and can be voluntarily surrendered.

The same is true of sovereignty over fiscal policy. Governments cannot finance, indefinitely, unsustainable budget deficits through global capital markets – though they can still coerce their citizens to lend to them through forced savings or monetary seigniorage and can default on both internal and external debt should they wish to do so. Paradoxically, globalization may have increased national discretion by enabling governments with fiscal deficits to borrow more widely in international markets.

There is, moreover, a wide variety of preferences for different levels and types of taxation even among open market economies, ranging from 70 per cent of the GDP accounted for by public spending in Sweden to 20 per cent in Singapore. The influence of globalization on economic management is real but usually subtle: operating through ideas of 'best practice' – as with rating agencies and competitiveness league tables – and peer group pressure among policy-making elites.

National sovereignty may also be eroded through the mobility of capital and 'human capital' and through trade liberalization. The location of production (and individuals with high net worth), and, to a degree, income distribution are affected by factor mobility and trade. When there is pressure on governments to counter these forces, national policy instruments no longer seem to work, or are unavailable. High corporate taxes and high tax rates on high incomes can lead to capital outflow and emigration. Exchange controls have been largely abandoned in developed countries and can be easily evaded, as is demonstrated by the magnitude of capital flight from countries which retain them. Controls on emigration by tax exiles and mobile individuals are difficult to enforce, at least in democratic societies. Trade controls are easier to deploy though there is new strong peer group pressure against them, at least in the OECD world. Large indirect tax differentials create arbitrage opportunities for smugglers. Tariffs are limited as revenue sources by freedom of trade.

In these various ways 'globalization' does inhibit governments' freedom of manoeuvre in economic policy but it does not eliminate it. Governments can do much to make their economies more or less attractive to investors: by supporting infrastructure development, education and training; increasing the efficiency and lowering the cost of services through competition or regulatory change; and improving the workings of labour markets.

There is, moreover, one key respect in which the nation-state still holds sway in a very direct way. Control over *population movements* is applied everywhere either through immigration control or population registration and monitoring. While there is evasion, and problems over refugees, large population movements of the kind which characterized the last century have largely been stopped and the pressures to exercise even tighter control over citizenship and residence are growing – perhaps because it is one domain in which traditional ideas of borders and territory can be effectively applied (Anderson, 1996).

The main thrust of the discussion above has been to underplay the rhetoric of globalization: to emphasize the ways in which states do and can, or might, continue to exercise real sovereign functions. In some cases – the definition of citizenship and enforcing the territorial basis of citizenship – globalization has made little impact.

Even recognizing that we are far from a 'borderless' globalized world, the role of nation-states has nonetheless changed in several quite fundamental ways. First, while governments retain independent instruments to attract and retain mobile capital or to pursue independent economic policies, their role has shifted from control through regulation to regulatory competition. In other words, systems of regulation are no longer nationally self-contained but have to be adapted for a world in which financial and human capital is footloose. Instruments of what may once have been exclusively domestic policy – education, social security, labour relations, corporate taxation, corporate governance, utilities regulation, systems of monetary management, law enforcement – are all new ingredients in 'competitiveness' and are constrained by it.

Second, nation-states find it increasingly difficult to perform (and therefore meet popular expectations) in some of their core functions. Income distribution is potentially affected by the asymmetry in the freedom to move between capital and labour and skilled and unskilled labour, by constraints on tax rates, social welfare systems and labour market regulation imposed by regulatory competition and possibly by trade. The Blair government's preference for low direct tax rates and reduced corporation tax is in substantial part conditioned by international realities. But again, it is necessary not to exaggerate. The Netherlands and Denmark – both open and successful economies – have more egalitarian societies than the more closed US. The evidence on trends in income distribution is also ambiguous.

But nonetheless, closer economic integration is bound to have implications for income distribution when endowments of human and capital resources are very unevenly spread. Governments may also struggle to meet popular expectations about personal security, which is affected by increasing change and competition whether originating in technology or international integration or the interaction between them. Nation-state governments are faced with a fundamental paradox: their legitimacy and effective operation depends on maintaining a degree of social cohesion and consensus; but the deeper international integration made possible by their successful performance may in turn undermine them. It is not surprising that there are politicians turning against the system and finding a ready market for nationalistic rhetoric.

National politics is inevitably affected by these changes. To be sure there is, as yet, no 'global' politics – except in weak institutions like the European Parliament. And there is far greater pluralism of political than economic regimes. While almost every state now has a (sort of) market economy, political regimes range from communism in China and Cuba, theocracy in Iran, absolute monarchy in Brunei and Oman to secular democracy in western Europe, America, Japan and India. Yet there is some indication that politics is increasingly difficult to contain within nation-state assumptions: many states are affected by the 'politics of identity', with large segments claiming allegiances to sub-national (tribal, regional) or pan-national (religious, linguistic) or other ethnic entities (see Cable, 1994), an issue pursued in the final section of this chapter. In this sense 'globalization' is having all-pervasive consequences.

Gainers and losers

One of the key conclusions of the economics of trade liberalization (and economic liberalization more widely) is that it is not a zero-sum game. There are benefits from specialization, scale competition and the diffusion of technology and good practice in which all can share. But the standard models already discussed also show how trade liberalization shifts distribution of income against labour, or specifically unskilled labour, in capital-rich countries and against capital in capital-scarce countries. There will also be adjustment costs from temporary unemployment and relocation or the closure of plants under conditions of intensified competition. A mountain of economic literature will demonstrate that the gains from liberalization invariably outweigh the costs; but costs and losers there are. Losers and prospective losers cannot be expected passively to accept losses, which is why 'globalization' is a controversial concept: a rallying point for opposition in countries as diverse as France, Japan, India and Mexico.

The most obvious casualties are those sectors that were previously most insulated from external competition, particularly some parts of agriculture. French arable farmers and Japanese and Korean rice farmers led opposition to the Uruguay Round liberalization. Indian farm lobbies have fiercely resisted opening up Indian agriculture to competition from foreign agribusiness and imports – even though studies show that many food and non-food farmers would benefit considerably from greater openness (Gulati, 1993). The alleged impact of NAFTA liberalization on the Mexican '*ejido*' maize grower was said to be a cause of the Zapatista uprising. The benefits to large numbers of poor people from access to cheaper staple food is no consolation to those driven from the land. The arguments advanced in the nineteenth-century debate over the Corn Laws have echoes today in Asia, in Latin America and, not least, in continental Europe.

Another powerful interest group is that of organized, predominantly unskilled, labour in rich countries which feels threatened by the migration of footloose capital to low-wage countries or by direct competition from imports. In the US, a movement reflecting these concerns, articulated by Ross Perot and Ralph Nader and marshalled by Congressman Gephardt, almost stopped the Mexico–NAFTA agreement being signed. It is currently blocking free trade agreements with the rest of Latin America and is a fearsome force in any policy debate involving trade with low-wage economies. There is, as noted above, a theoretical basis for concern about the impact of north–south trade on unskilled labour in rich countries though the theory is static in character and most research shows the impact to be small. The empirical evidence recently pulled together by Robert Lawrence (1994) suggests that changes in demand patterns (to services from manufacturers) and relatively rapid productivity growth in manufacturing in the US have been far more important than trade in explaining the growing gap between college-educated workers and those who cease education when they leave school and will remain so under any plausible set of assumptions. But the debate coincides with a long period of stagnation in blue-collar wages in the US and rising income inequality and it is easy to blame foreigners. Much of the support for protectionism in the US Congress derives from blue-collar workers. In western Europe, rising unemployment rather than falling wages is the problem and is frequently invoked against both immigration and import competition (Goldsmith, 1996).

Another set of losers comprises indigenous, protected, capitalists (including state capitalists) facing external competition for the first time. Fierce resistance to 'globalization' has been mounted by Swadeshi ('homespun') capitalists in India who fear competition with their weak local brands. Many Indian – like Chinese – family businesses are proving robust in the face of multinational competition and some have skilfully established alliances and joint ventures to survive. Nonetheless indigenous business provides much of the backbone to populist nationalist campaigns against foreign investors and imports.

Local communities are often the fiercest source of resistance to change, which is often attributed to globalization (Jones, 1997; Julius, 1997). Any form of disruptive upheaval threatens the networks of friendship and neighbourliness which, for many, especially the elderly, are as important for the quality of life as national advance and widening choice and opportunities. Anyone familiar with local politics will know the immense passion generated by apparently innocuous proposals to change planning use, change a bus route, build a block of houses or cut down a tree. Globalization not merely speeds up change but increases the visibility of strangers and their activities and the impact of mobile companies which are difficult to hold to account, can simply walk away from troublesome local problems or make proposals on a 'take it or leave it' basis. In the more conservative societies, generalized resentment at the changes produced by globalization should not be underestimated and may well contribute further to the growth of extreme-right movements in France, Austria, Italy and elsewhere.

The beneficiaries of globalization are likely to be much more numerous than the losers but perhaps less aware of the diffuse benefits they enjoy. Consumers, everywhere, have access to greater choice and lower costs (unless competition involves predation and leads to monopoly). Companies – and their shareholders and employees – can seek out new markets and lower costs and enjoy greater economies of scale. Workers in poor countries have greater opportunities as a result of their employers' access to overseas markets (and, to a limited degree, opportunities to migrate overseas). Despite the emotive campaigning literature about the 'exploitation' of labour in low-wage exporting countries, much of the research points to improving real wages and conditions (Kreuger, 1978; Bhagwati, 1998; World Bank, 1993) even in craft industries where child labour is common (Cable, Jain and Weston, 1983).

The gain and loss equation will, in practice, often have more to do with the particularities of a specific market structure than global integration in the round. Globalization produces intense competition as well as wider opportunities. Shipping lines and shipbuilding, civil airlines, chemicals and steel have all been subject to serious profitability crises. Traditional commodities including cocoa, bananas, coffee and tea have been 'globalized' since the days of the Romans, if not earlier; but they have suffered declining commodity terms of trade for many years owing to oversupply. Access to global markets is no guarantee of success.

Globalization gives the biggest advantages to those who can play on a global stage but are shielded from all-out competition by a unique brand (Coca-Cola, Gucci), patented standard (Gates' MS-DOS), star appeal (Pavarotti's voice; Madonna's sexuality) or star product (Elvis memorabilia; Cantona shirts), copyright allied to brand (Disney), or semi-monopolistic position built up from technological advantages, scale and negotiated rights (Murdoch; Time-Warner; CNN). Globalization is opening up a big gulf in earning power between the limited pool of those in any trade or profession with recognized – global – star quality and run-of-the-mill performers. This phenomenon is observable in sport (the gap between Premier League or Serie A footballers and their fellow players), the arts, science, popular music, merchant banking, journalism, fiction, and business management. In a globalized economy in which proprietary knowledge (in the widest sense) is a scarce resource and a major source of value, rewards accrue to those individuals or companies that can exploit its scarcity value globally – a value created through a brand or patent or copyright or simply by reputation. In such a world, financial rewards also accrue to a globally recognized mark of quality: a Harvard

MBA; a good Oxbridge or Ecole Poytechnique first degree; a professional qualification at the Delft School of Mines; an Oscar award; an 1SO 9000; even a favourable mention in the *Financial Times* or *Wall Street Journal.* Globalization thus rewards the many but also a few in particular. The disparities in rewards, thus produced, have enormous implications for domestic politics, feeding the politics of envy, and creating a new class of individuals and companies with exceptional leverage.

Beyond economics: national security

Globalization also makes increasingly redundant some national security functions of the state. Such is the degree of economic interdependence, at least among Western countries, that traditional warfare between them is virtually inconceivable. We should perhaps be careful not to slide into hubris since the world of 1913 was also highly integrated. But the world now is qualitatively quite different, with extensive cross-border integrated production and the nationality of companies an increasingly meaningless concept. The ideological struggle between East and West has almost entirely ceased. Moreover the motive of conflict to secure physical resources has ceased to be an issue in a world where leading economies are knowledge- rather than industry-based, except for the oil-producing Gulf. There are states where politicians do provide a traditional function of mobilizing the population to defend itself against enemies and to fight – India and Pakistan, or Israel, would be examples – but in modern Western countries subject to high degrees of economic integration this role has largely disappeared. Fighting is a specialized profession.

Globalization has, however, contributed to a fresh set of 'security' problems, not easily dealt with through national political mobilization. The first relates to the difficulties in an open world economy of containing the dissemination of advanced military technology. The number of states with nuclear weapons, chemical and germ weapons and intercontinental ballistic missile capability rises steadily. The difficulties of limiting the military technology of a small country such as Iraq, despite global sanctions and military defeat, are a poignant reminder of the problem. In a world where defence industries are encouraged to emulate commercial enterprise and develop trade and overseas investment opportunities, leakage of military technology is profuse. The former COCOM trade control regime, which kept the most sophisticated technologies from the USSR during the Cold War, is very difficult to apply in a more globally integrated world where potential enemies are less clearly defined. Problems of this kind require cooperative solutions and strong global governance (Cable, 1995).

A second set of problems concerns terrorism. Much contemporary terrorism is perpetrated by organizations representing dissident nationality or ethnic groups; this in turn reflects the breaking down of the nation-state as the source of temporal loyalty. Terrorist activities are relatively easy to coordinate in a world with good communications. And an internationally integrated economy also offers juicy targets such as airports or financial centres (both London and Bombay have been bombed) or tourist haunts. A major outrage can achieve publicity around the globe for an otherwise obscure group. Within a short time there may well be groups with an international network of cells and in possession of weapons of mass destruction. Traditional national security structures are of limited value. Terrorism, as much as any other phenomenon, is forcing governments into habits of international cooperation.

A third problem, related in many ways, could be called 'trade in bads'. As barriers to commerce and freedom of movement come down, it becomes more difficult to stop traffic in goods, or services, which some or all governments want to outlaw: drugs, pornography (now available on the Internet and through telephone services as well as in print form) and the laundering of money associated with crime. Those who have studied international crime argue that the leading gangs – among the Colombian cartels, the Italian Mafia, the Triads – operate like highly efficient multinational businesses with well-developed but flexible management structures, excellent global communication networks, joint ventures and corporate alliances, carefully cultivated relationships with suppliers, subcontractors and distributors and, above all, a feel for markets. Government agencies sent to fight them are doubly disadvantaged in the era of globalization by the inhibitions of public-sector bureaucracy and by a national rather than international perspective. As with terrorism, this is a fertile ground for rapid, forced, learning in the habits of international cooperation.

Lastly, there is the problem of migration. We have already noted above that this is one of the exceptions to the general trend towards closer integration. European countries may have recently experienced immigration, from outside western Europe, on a scale on a scale unfamiliar to earlier generations, but the immigrant minorities are rarely a large proportion of the total population and primary immigration has been largely stopped. The US is much more open to immigration than any other developed country, but flows are not large compared with a century ago and serious attempts are being made to stop them. The US Border Patrol budget has tripled in five years. Immigration control has become an issue in Japan (in reaction to a very small influx from Asia), Singapore (where measures are draconian) the Gulf (where immigration minorities are proportionately large but subject to discriminatory treatment and close surveillance) and in the Indian subcontinent (a barbed fence is being constructed around the entire frontier of Bangladesh). Migration is one of the few aspects of globalization which governments can effectively control on a territorial basis (people being more detectable than electrons), and there are strong political demands that they should do so on grounds of national identity, despite economic costs. In many cases the defence of national frontiers – security in the traditional sense – no longer has anything to do with invading armies but is largely concerned with the policing of migration.

The redundancy of traditional forms of national security has led to attempts to reinvent the language of national security for a world of economic globalization, in particular the use of the concept of 'economic security' to dramatize temporary imbalances in trade or current account as acts of calculated aggression, noticeably by Japan, against the USA (Thurow, 1993; Luttwak, 1994). This crude and dated mercantilism has been stilled for the time being by the obvious difficulties of the Japanese economy, relative to the US. But the growing imbalances in trade between East Asia and the US (and the EU) will very probably lead to a revival of this kind of political debate, deploying 'national security' arguments in the economic field, however speciously.

What complicates the interrelationship between globalization and national security is that not all nation-states are at the same stage of integration with the global system (Cooper, 1996). Cooper helpfully distinguishes three basic stages. In one, that of the so-called developed countries and many of the smaller and more open developing countries and some of the transition countries of eastern Europe, globalization is advanced, apparently irreversible and accepted as a major constraint on what nation-states can do. A second encompasses those countries that are still consolidating their positions as nation-states in much the same way as, say, Germany or Italy at the end of the nineteenth century. They have a recent history of conflict with neighbours; a tendency to see international relations in traditional balance-of-power terms; and limited integration with the outside world. China, India, Iran, Indonesia and the new Russia and Ukraine would be good examples. A third stage comprises the weak states of – mainly – Africa where national identity is weak but international integration is limited by poverty and the marginalization of the population from modern communications. This categorization is over-stylized and simplified but broadly correct. Globalization means something different in the different groups of countries. For the first there is general political acceptance that traditional nation-state functions have changed radically and there is a search for mechanisms to manage deep integration. For the second, the political environment is one where there is shallow global integration largely through trade and foreign investment but also a strong 'national' politics built around serious conflict with neighbours over territory. For the third, political activity is frequently limited to securing a tenuous grip on power.

The politics of identity

The way in which national politics functions is being radically changed by globalization: most fundamentally, the nature of underlying political discourse. Most political debate has traditionally centred on Left or Right issues: the desirability and extent of state as opposed to private ownership; the role of markets as against state controls; organized labour versus business and its allies; degrees of redistribution and universal welfare. These issues still exist, of course, but the range of argument has greatly narrowed. Socialism as a system of economic organization has been largely discredited. There is a broad consensus on the merits of economic liberalization. Former Communist parties share, and implement, that consensus. Privatization, balanced budgets, sound money, a welcome mat for foreign investment: these have been enthusiastically endorsed or accepted with weary resignation across the political spectrum: by Italian, Chinese and Vietnamese Communists, French Socialists, Peronists, European Social Democrats, Iranian mullahs and South African nationalist revolutionaries.

While the Left–Right dimension of politics has narrowed, politics continues nonetheless. In some cases – the US, the UK, Germany – democratic politics has become more personalized and concerned with style; in others, as in India, there are shifting coalitions of interest groups without any clear ideological thread.

An ideological vacuum has also been created in which a new kind of political polarization exists around the 'politics of identity' (Figure 2.1): the politics of religion (the Christian Coalition in the US; Hindu 'fundamentalism' in India; Islamic movements in Turkey, North Africa, Egypt), language (Canada, Belgium, India again), regional nationalism (Catalonia, Scotland, Padania) or race (the National Front in France, the

Figure 2.1: The new politics of identity

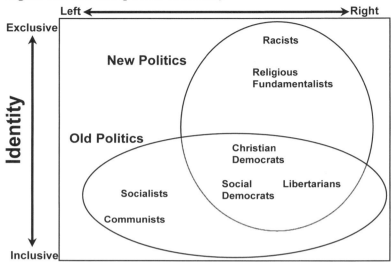

Source: Cable, 1994.

People's Party in Austria, Hansen's New Australia Party). Globalization has contributed to the process by facilitating mass communications in vernacular languages among minorities and diasporas. Some of these political forces further weaken the authority of the nation-state by emphasizing the identity, and sovereign rights, of ethnic and other minorities, and also international movements, such as Islam.

But it is already evident that the new politics of identity can also be turned into a force of reaction against economic integration. Indian Hindu nationalist politicians have sought to mobilize opinion not just against Muslims (and foreign workers) but against multinational companies too. The submerged ethnic and religious identities of Southeast Asia are assuming, in Malaysia for example, a generally xenophobic form. Even in the world's remaining superpower, incipient isolationism and economic protectionism is being reinforced by antipathy to Mexicans and East Asians.

The politics of antipathy to globalization may deploy nationalism and the politics of identity. But it may also draw on environmentalism (the British Green Party, albeit a negligible force at present, has embraced the 'New Protectionism') and traditional concerns of the Left for social cohesion and equality (Gray, 1993).

These concerns are at present largely expressed on the political margins but a period of economic crisis could radically change the climate of opinion. The attempt of Malaysia's Dr Mahathir, for example, to regain political legitimacy by invoking economic nationalism has wider lessons.

For national politics to come to terms with globalization some major changes have to occur:

- effective global governance to cope with market failures and cross-border co-operation;
- measures to ensure that the international public sector – institutions and regulators – are democratically accountable;
- a clear sense of subsidiarity such that national (and sub-national) politics enjoy maximum decentralization of decision-making within global or regional rules.

Many of the most vigorous debates now taking place about international institutions – the powers of the European Commission and Community agencies; the IMF; the MAI – essentially revolve around these questions. The remaining chapters try to address these issues.

Chapter 3

Managing the system

An evolving system

Popular denigration of the current international economic system as 'global *laissez- faire*' (Gray, 1993) obscures half a century of efforts to develop institutions and rules for an increasingly integrated system. It was recognized by the founders of the international economic postwar order that international structures were necessary to promote trade and prevent another relapse into protectionism; to stimulate economic development; to ease balance-of-payments adjustment; and (though this was never realized) to stabilize commodity prices (Vines, 1997).

As shown in Table 3.1, the system of governance has evolved in several ways:

- a big increase in complexity: more institutions and more institutional overlap, with regional and global arrangements;
- new sets of problems, notably those associated with the liberalization of capital flows and the environment;
- a greater emphasis on market self-regulation in capital markets, standard-setting and network management.

What are the limitations of these arrangements? Is there a 'regulatory deficit'? In the recent climate of perceived crisis there have been many advocates of stronger international policy coordination or institutions (Carlsson and Ramphal, 1993). But there is also a contrary argument: that there is regulatory overload rather than deficit at a global level and that financial instability has been caused by inappropriate rather than insufficient intervention.

Table 3.1: The development of global governance

Identified externality	Postwar	Now
Macroeconomic management spillovers/coordination	IMF(Adjustable peg system)	G7 European Union/EMU (OECD)(IMF)
Rules for promoting liberal trade	GATT	WTO Regional customs unions and free trade areas
Rules for direct foreign investment	(UN)	WTO OECD European Union World Bank (MIGA)
Systemic stability for capital markets and international banking	(Exchange controls)	Self-regulation (IOSCO) BIS (IMF) (IIF)
Economic development	World Bank (UN)	World Bank IMF Regional banks
International environmental spillovers and agreements	UN agencies and ILO	UN agencies (e.g. UNEP and WMO) Regional agreements
Standard setting		Self-regulation ISO Regional agreements (EU Single Market) (WTO) (UN agencies)
Network management	UN agencies (ICAO; WMO; ITU)	Internet UN agencies plus private self-regulation
Commodity price stability	(UN – commodity control)	Regional agreements Self-regulation (OPEC)

The broad questions subsume more specific issues. In which particular areas – such as systemic risk – is there a regulatory deficit? If there is to be more developed global governance, which governments and institutions should play a bigger role? How should some of the emerging issues – regulatory competition; Internet traffic; extraterritoriality; ethical trade and investment practices – be incorporated into global governance? This chapter will describe the system as it currently operates; the next will try to address these questions in more detail

Global rules for deeper integration

Free trade has long been a rallying slogan for those favouring (or opposing) closer economic integration. The battle is far from over for liberalization. Powerful lobbies have prevented much headway being made in some sectors, especially in agriculture. As noted above, countries such as China and India have done little more than dip their toes in the waters of international competition and there are serious obstacles, still, to China and Russia being admitted to membership of the World Trade Organization. Complaints about 'unfair' Japanese trading practices linger, especially in the US.

Yet it is becoming clear with hindsight that the early 1990s marked a fundamental turning point in respect of trade policy. The Uruguay Round trade agreements were delayed, and weakened by compromises, but succeeded in the end. They contained a crucial step in global economic governance: a structure for dispute settlement which allowed, in the last resort, a multinational panel to rule against national governments. Despite US opposition (and a condition under the US Trade Act that US 'national interests' must not be overridden more than three times), the system is now working. It is currently being invoked against US unilateral action in relation to Japan (where Japan has been supported by the EU), by the US against the EU (bananas; meat hormones) and by all Western countries against India (to make India speed up its removal of quantitative import restrictions). Implicit in these developments is an acceptance that sovereignty has to be surrendered if rules to promote liberalization are to be credible.

Another fundamental change has been in the type of problem with which global economic governance is concerned. One of the key factors leading to deepening integration has been the growth of capital flows and pressures for rules to embrace them. The Uruguay Round also broke new ground in creating a framework of multilateral rules for foreign investment, recognizing that FDI, rather than trade, is now at the cutting edge of globalization. There is a limited agreement on trade-related investment measures (TRIMS) such as content rules; an agreement (TRIPS) requiring national protection of intellectual property in order to allow trade and investment with embodied knowledge to take place; and a framework agreement to liberalize 'trade' in non-traded services, according investors equal, 'national', treatment in host countries.

A third change of comparable importance has been the creation of rules for deepening integration at regional level. The Uruguay Round agreement came to fruition at the same time as the creation of the European Single Market in 1992. Like the Uruguay Round, the Single Market initially inspired only modest enthusiasm and met seemingly impossible obstacles of sectional and national interest. It eventually succeeded with a dawning realization that closer economic integration was no longer a matter of removing trade barriers but of addressing the obstacles to trade and investment created by numerous, customary, national regulatory practices. There is now a great deal of anecdotal data on the large costs imposed on commerce by divergent regulations – for example, in multiple production lines for the same products, testing delays and costs (OECD, 1997). Some regulation, of course, serves social, environmental, health and safety and other policy objectives but it presents problems for international trade when it is discriminatory (against foreigners), more restrictive than necessary for its objectives, dictated by national vested interests and non-transparent.

Some harmonization of standards now occurs not only at a regional but at a global level in the BIS (with minimum banking standards), the ISO and its many sector-specific standards bodies, the WTO (the Index Alimentarius on health standards for food) and in the TRIPS agreement. But harmonization is often difficult and slow when large numbers of governments are involved and the issues are technically complex. There have been major failures (electric sockets; TV and video).

In practice, deepening of integration through harmonization of standards and regulations has largely been an EU rather than a global development. A key breakthrough was the realization in the EU that trying to harmonize tens of thousands of regulations between twelve, then fifteen, countries was a hopeless task and fraught with debilitating political aggravation (as in the endless British scare stories about compulsory square tomatoes, hairnets for fishermen and the abolition of double-decker buses). Instead, a more permissive form of deregulation was adopted: the mutual recognition of different national regulatory systems or, put simply, the idea that British beer should be acceptable in Germany; Greek accountants in Britain; and Italian skis in Finland. This apparently blindingly obvious idea (combined with a degree of full harmonization) has been accepted with some difficulty but has made the Single Market possible and is beginning to be applied on a global scale. The next regional achievement was the NAFTA free trade agreement between the US and Mexico, despite opposition in both those countries. Its importance lay in the acceptance of beneficial integration between a rich and a poor country: one labour scarce, one labour-abundant. All the classic prejudices – well-paid workers being 'undercut' by cheap 'sweated' labour; the 'giant sucking sound' to the South; 'neo-imperialist exploitation' of the poor by the rich – had to be confronted. The demand of the US for minimum labour and environmental standards has been accommodated (to the alarm of many free traders) but in a way which has not in practice resulted in protectionist trade restrictions. It is premature to claim that the project is a success – and its extension to other countries is being resisted in the US – but, politically and economically, new ground was broken.

Lastly, there has been an attempt, through APEC, to introduce some rules and trade liberalization targets among the disparate economies of Asia and the Pacific basin. The significance here is that it brings into a formal, liberalizing, framework those countries which might otherwise be prone to conflict over economic (and security) matters: the US, China and Japan and others differing enormously in wealth and economic history. It also, for the first time, introduces rules into a regime where integration has occurred mainly thorough FDI rather than trade.

These agreements can be seen as the first tranche of a much bigger set of proposals designed to create global rules for competition regardless of whether this originates in cross-border sales or overseas investment. The preparatory ideas for a new round of trade negotiations – the Millennium Round – under the WTO include a fully-fledged international competition policy, rules for investment incentives going beyond trade-related measures and disciplines over corporate taxation, national treatment of foreign investment in general, standards related to corporate governance and such politically charged subjects as business corruption. In a world where FDI flows are growing rapidly, neglect of these subjects will create sources of conflict since, in the absence of rules, companies will suffer capricious and discriminatory treatment and conflicts of laws will arise as major countries seek to impose rules extraterritorially.

The central point is that change from trade-related to investment-related problems is not just technical but involves a deeper paradigm. It involves a redefinition of what 'national sovereignty' means in a globally integrated world.

International rules and national sovereignty

Globalization – particularly its most advanced manifestations in financial markets, information industries and corporate networks – has radical implications for the traditional view of international relations. The traditional view can be caricatured as one of solid nation-states interacting through trade or military alliances but without significant loss of sovereignty (Bull, 1997). The model of 'billiard ball' interactions has been used to describe the way self-contained nation-states, each a separate political community, relate to one another. This model could be first seen in the Europe which emerged from the Treaty of Westphalia in 1648 and, despite periods of war, colonialism and revolutionary upheaval, provides many of the underlying assumptions behind international relations to this day. Much of the current excitement about 'loss of sovereignty' – in relation to the EU, or in the US in relation to global institutions – reflects a sense of dismay that this world appears to be disappearing.

Until recently it was possible to combine a commitment to an advanced degree of international – global and regional – economic integration through freedom of trade and investment (and, even, labour movements) with a strong commitment to the political centrality of the nation-state. The nineteenth-century, pre-1914, world was one in which an advanced system of international economic integration evolved within a framework dominated by competing states. In modern times Margaret Thatcher has been perhaps the most articulate representative of this total separation between the economic and political domains.

The postwar order, to some degree, still respects such a distinction: a liberal economic system, albeit largely restricted to the developed Western world, operated by independent, but cooperating, nation-states. The apex public-sector agency, the United Nations, is not and never has been a supranational organization; it can proceed no further or faster than its member states – some doubly protected by vetoes – will let it. The GATT, despite the success of its rounds of negotiations, never had – until the Uruguay Round – the supranational authority to impose dispute settlement procedures. The Bretton Woods institutions came closer to such a supranational authority though they are quite closely controlled by governments, particularly their main shareholders. Even in the field of the 'global commons' – geographical space which no nation-state 'owns' – there has been an encroachment rather than withdrawal of national sovereignty (such as the 200-mile territorial limits under the Law of the Sea) or, at best, a freezing of national territorial claims (as in Antarctica).

It is only within the specific and localized case of the EU that sovereignty sharing – through majority voting and some degree of regulatory harmonization – has proceeded steadily to a point where some form of supranational governance is evolving. At the same time, elsewhere, the break-up of empires and multinational states has led to a proliferation of nation-states – from 44 in 1944 at the Bretton Woods conference to a number approaching 200 – all asserting their sovereignty. The era of globalization has also been the era of the nation-state. Or so it seems.

Globalization has, however, set in train a series of changes which shake to its foundations the idea of the national state. The clear boundaries between 'domestic' and 'foreign' policies have eroded. Large numbers of issues which were once seen as purely domestic are now influenced by events abroad: tax levels and structure; social security systems; product and technical standards; worker conditions; regulation of financial institutions; ownership of utilities; corporate governance and company law; environmental protection; competition policy; government budget deficits; education standards; human rights. Margaret Thatcher's pained complaint that 'Europe' was getting into the 'nooks and crannies' of British life would be echoed by politicians everywhere and not just about Europe. Negotiations between Japan and the US, initially over 'trade', have been extended into education, savings performance and the use of metrication. The process is a cumulative one. The more countries become economically integrated, the more aspects of national life are affected; and the greater the success in overcoming any frictions which result, the deeper integration can become.

To some degree, national differences in regulation shouldn't matter. The differences in the Scottish and English legal and education systems or in the tax or legal systems of US states do not affect high levels of economic integration even within countries. Regulatory systems can coexist or compete in a single market. Frictions arise, and domestic concerns become 'foreign' when there are 'spillovers' – of which there are several kinds. There are cross-border externalities. Cross-border (or global) pollution, from, say, CO_2 and SO_2 emissions, is an obvious example of how unconstrained national activity will have negative efforts elsewhere (and lead to friction). One country's financial and fiscal policies will also influence conditions overseas. This has become a key issue in the arguments for closer economic union in Europe (Currie and Whiteley, 1993); the argument is that since one country's macro-economic policies increasingly impact on another's, there should be some joint management or sovereignty pooling. Then, there is pressure to remove barriers to trade, or foreign investment, resulting from national regulatory devices, as in the EU Single Market: standards, for example, imposed for consumer protection but which may have the effect of discriminating against foreign suppliers. The Single Market has worked as a result of an acceptance of sovereignty pooling (through an extension of qualified majority voting) as being the only way to rid the EU of numerous national practices which would otherwise constitute barriers to trade.

A more contentious area where there may be limits to national autonomy and regulatory competition is in relation to 'fair competition'. In trade, there has been a long-standing, centuries-old, debate around the fact that while many of the benefits of trade derive from differences between countries – in the cost and availability of labour and resource endowments and consumer tastes – the same differences lead to complaints from domestic firms that there is not a 'level playing field'. Within the trading system there has evolved a broad consensus on differences that are not admissible (export subsidies supported by governments; classical dumping designed to achieve monopoly from predatory pricing). Intensified competition is now also bringing into question the legitimacy of cost differentials achieved, for example, through different environmental and labour standards as had already occurred in NAFTA. The serious argument is that there is not merely 'unfairness' (whatever that means) but an overall drop in standards arising from competition: a spillover effect. The search for 'fairness' may be a thinly disguised excuse for old-fashioned protectionism but it is also opening up important areas of national economies to external scrutiny.

The tendency to blur the distinction between national and foreign is reinforced by moves to create rules for foreign investment. The embryonic GATT services agreement incorporates the principle of national treatment for the first time. Governments are expected to treat domestic and foreign enterprises equally. Another area of national discretion is being increasingly called into question as a result of the Uruguay Round whereby governments have lost national discretion over the definition of intellectual property rights. Intellectual property rights must now meet standards which are not merely non-discriminatory but satisfy foreign investors and their home governments.

What is also emerging is a search for structures to manage regulatory competition where this gives one country a competitive advantage in attracting foreign investment or leads to a competitive 'race to the bottom' to attract mobile capital. The emerging literature on regulatory competition – discussed in more detail below – does not suggest that there are clear-cut spillovers in this area though there may be in some cases. For example, competition in investment incentives and corporate taxes could be leading to an overall shortfall in government revenue (and thus publicly financed collective provision). Weak banking regulations may enable fraudsters to continue to operate legally overseas and escape justice. Since there are few aspects of national economic and social policy which could not be brought within the general concept of regulatory competition, almost every aspect of national policy is potentially embraced by regimes designed to manage this competition.

Last, but not least, is the ethical dimension: the idea that an individual country's politics in its widest sense is the concern of people elsewhere because there is a common set of values. The implications for international governance are immense and are already being seen in attempts to influence environmental policy, individual human rights, animal rights, emigration policy, labour practices, birth control and abortion policy, the choice of political regimes, the rights of self-determination for minorities and much else using official trade and aid sanctions or informal consumer and private investor boycotts. Some of these patterns of behaviour may be wearily familiar in countries which have just emerged from colonial status or in weak states which have become used to having foreign aid donors or powerful neighbours define their domestic policy for them. But for international economic relations more generally to have to accommodate a wide set of common values would be revolutionary and totally demolish the old 'billiard ball' concept of international relations.

What globalization is leading to, therefore, is a world of new and increasingly intrusive international rules designed to open markets, contain or redress 'spillovers', create a sense of 'fairness' among competitors and reflect common values.

Global variable geometry

The system of global governance that is emerging as a response to globalization is a complex, often ad hoc, set of rules, regimes and institutions which go beyond traditional ideas of limited cooperation between nation states but so far fall short of a unified global system underpinned by global law enforcement. It is an untidy world with overlapping jurisdictions and competition between different kinds of rules and institutions (Figure 3.1).

There has been a movement away from traditional ideas of multilateral cooperation embodied in the United Nations and, to a lesser extent, the

Figure 3.1: World governance (1)

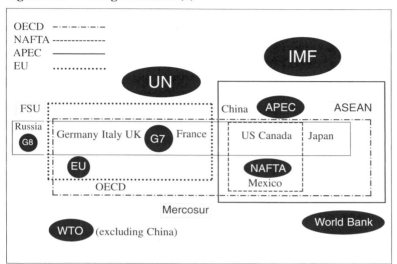

Source: Author.

Bretton Woods institutions and GATT. Because globalization is linked inextricably with ideas of liberalization, the new forms of governance emphasize private – rather than public – sector activity, including self-regulation; an ideologically committed – market-oriented – approach rather than one which is neutral; and a role for the international public sector which is not activist and interventionist and has more to do with facilitation and the provision of genuine public goods.

It is also possible to define and observe several different levels of commitment to international integration. These range from the shallowest form of integration in some form of limited free trade area association through to ambitious sovereignty sharing and acceptance of supranational authority, as with Economic and Monetary Union (EMU) and the European Central Bank.

EMU is the best example we have of co-sovereignty: the sharing of sovereignty over a major area of policy. In the EU it is not a unique step (Belgium and Luxembourg have long had a monetary union, and the Benelux countries have had a *de facto* monetary union among themselves and with Germany). EMU exemplifies the way in which closer integration generates a demand for stronger international governance, which in turn generates closer integration. Greater regional trade ran into obstacles

55

Figure 3.2: Progress towards European integration

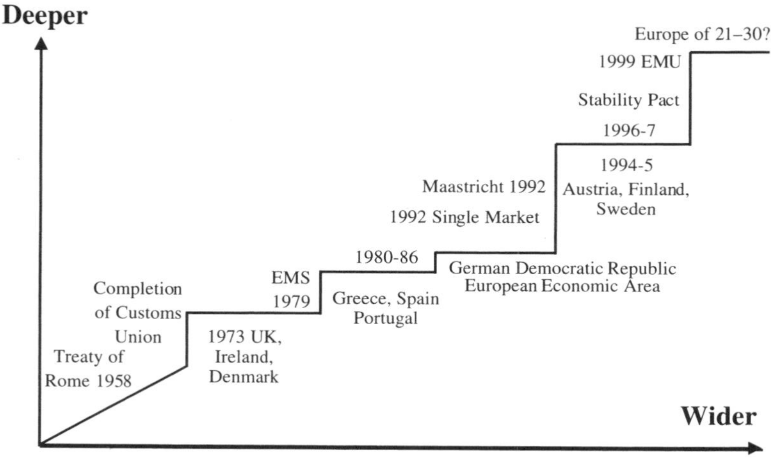

Deeper

Europe of 21–30?

1999 EMU

Stability Pact
1996-7

1994-5
Maastricht 1992   Austria, Finland,
1992 Single Market   Sweden

1980-86   German Democratic Republic
EMS   European Economic Area
Completion   1979   Greece, Spain
of Customs   Portugal
Union   1973 UK,
Treaty of   Ireland,
Rome 1958   Denmark

Wider

Source: Albert Bressand (Prométhée).

created by different national product standards, which has in turn led to single market liberalization. The full benefits of a single market were in turn seen as more likely to be realized when costs and prices were fully transparent across the market as a whole and companies could conduct their marketing and production planning within the same economic envelope. Closer integration has magnified macroeconomic spillovers, leading in turn to demands for closer policy coordination – including common monetary policy and also currency stability. EMU will in turn accelerate capital and labour market integration which will then speed up agreed rules to facilitate both. There are legitimate arguments for and against pressing ahead with the project in its present form. But the evolutionary logic is inescapable. As Figure 3.2 shows, EMU has not emerged suddenly, but represents the culmination of thirty years or more of preparation with steps alternately widening and deepening the European Union.

The degree of sovereignty pooling, or co-sovereignty, under EMU should be neither minimized nor exaggerated. Each state will share in the management of the European Central Bank, which will in turn operate according to principles agreed in advance, emphasizing a low-inflation objective. Some member states will acquire an element of additional sovereignty. The Benelux countries and (arguably) France, which had adopted a Deutschmark currency peg and were thereby tied to German monetary policy will now have a formal, and real, stake in the management of European monetary policy. Sovereignty will be surrendered primarily by Germany which will, in effect, share its hitherto exclusive management of the Bundesbank.

The other major area of sovereignty pooling within EMU is in fiscal policy with adoption of the solidarity pact limiting fiscal deficit to 2 per cent of GDP with some leeway in times of recession (but fines for persistent delinquency). However, the loss of sovereignty in adopting the solidarity pact is less significant than it appears. There is provision to vary policy over the cycle. There is little constraint on the overall level and mix of taxation and public spending, though there is a separate debate over how much tax harmonization is necessary for a single market in goods and savings. The alternative taskmasters of fiscal policy, moreover, are not national governments but global bond markets. In a globalized world economy, full fiscal sovereignty is increasingly illusory. The essence of co-sovereignty is that governments consciously share and assert sovereignty over areas of policy where policy discretion is, in any event, being severely circumscribed by the impersonal forces of market globalization. EMU is exploring a route which other groups of countries may well follow.

Another element in the complexities of the integration process is the emergence of sub-national units of government as important players. This derives in part from the fact that nation-states are pushing ahead with commitments to international economic integration which can be more advanced than domestic integration. China is negotiating within the WTO and the Asia-Pacific Economic Community (APEC) to dismantle domestic trade barriers, though these remain on internal trade. Indeed one of the more difficult issues in the negotiations is the fact that different provinces pursue different trade policies. The problem arises not only in relation to new players. The German *Länder* were constitutionally required to endorse the GATT Uruguay Round agreement. And as international integration is increasingly concerned with investment flows and regulatory competition among authorities, the complexities introduced by federal states (the US, Canada, Germany, Russia, China, India, Brazil) are very great. One set of regulations may be established by local authorities – zoning, for example; another by provincial bodies – some taxes and incentives or infrastructure; and yet another by national governments – competition policy, other taxes.

The postwar vision of multinational cooperation envisaged strong global governance institutions with near-universal membership such as the UN, GATT, the IMF and the World Bank. These institutions are struggling now to cope with the different expectations among their large membership with different degrees of commitment to deeper integration and with many potential claims on limited management capacity. There are various different institutional life forms evolving as part of the new variable geometry.

(A) Intergovernmental clubs
One response has been the formation of a series of voluntary clubs of nation-states. The characteristic of clubs is that they voluntarily share rights and duties without coercion. Free-riding is eliminated by restricting benefits to members. The clubs come into existence because there is some public good which will not be provided by competing private firms or individual nation-states acting in isolation.

As a way of organizing international affairs, clubs have advantages of flexibility, and they provide a practical solution to 'public goods' problems which might otherwise wait indefinitely for a truly global solution. There is, however, a constant need for calculation as to whether the benefits of exclusive cooperation exceed the costs of expanding membership or of undisciplined behaviour by an excluded potential member. In some cases the calculation has been that it is better to have a wide membership without discrimination than short cuts more easily achievable by an exclusive group. GATT (and now the WTO), for example, has established non-discrimination as a cardinal principle, which would be breached if like-minded countries were to press ahead with liberalization among themselves alone.

Some clubs have only modest objectives and only a few, weak, rules. *Clubs of influence* such as the OECD and the Commonwealth are concerned with influencing the climate of opinion through intergovernmental dialogue. They facilitate rather than act. Membership may confer few tangible benefits but is nonetheless tenaciously pursued (Mexico and the OECD) or fiercely defended (Nigeria and the Commonwealth). While there is some cynicism about the role played by intergovernmental bodies of this kind ('talking shop' is a common epithet) they have come into their own as a bridge between governments which want to communicate in less formal ways than in the UN system, and as a trailer for more substantial negotiations (as in APEC; and, potentially, the transatlantic 'dialogue').

Some clubs aspire to a wider role in policy coordination. The G7 was founded on the basis that since its members accounted for over half the world's GDP they could effectively capture most of the benefits of policy coordination. These benefits include reducing the risks of trade warfare and unwanted macroeconomic spillovers, averting systemic collapse – arising from the weakness of the banking system in the early 1980s – and minimizing the impact of such shocks as the 1980/81 oil shock and the 1987 stock market collapse. The G7 – or now the G8, including Russia as a partial member – has not evolved fast enough to incorporate some of the major emerging players, notably China. Critics argue that it has generated few benefits from policy coordination and may have led to damaging mistakes (as at the 'reflationary' 1978 Bonn summit). The existence of such a club has, however, almost certainly contributed to habits of cooperation; it has prevented some important players being excluded and scapegoated – Japan, for example; and it has promoted a venue for some important initiatives, as with the 1998 coordinated approach to interest-rate cuts.

(B) Regional clubs
The pressures for regional, rather than global, integration have been described above. Projects designed to promote regional integration have proved extremely popular in recent years. There have been well over 100 notified to GATT since 1947 (under the Article 24 exemption from the Most Favoured Nation clause) and over 30 since 1990. Intra-regional trade (which does not, however, necessarily depend upon the existence of formal integration arrangements) accounts for an all-time high of just over 50 per cent of world trade – as against 33 per cent in 1948 and 37 per cent in 1938.

The groupings vary enormously in type and effectiveness. Most of the regional clubs formed among developing countries in Africa, Latin America and the Middle East to promote import substitution at regional level and highly circumscribed regional free trade have foundered. Regional integration in the communist bloc has been reversed with the collapse of COMECON and the USSR.

The institutional architecture which has emerged is described impressionistically in Figure 3.3. Three main regional associations – of quite different kinds – are loosely linked with one another through trans-regional associations (APEC; the Trans-Atlantic Partnership (TAP)) and global institutions (the WTO), and contain a hierarchy of members. By far the most important of the regional clubs is the EU whose internal

Figure 3.3: Regionalism

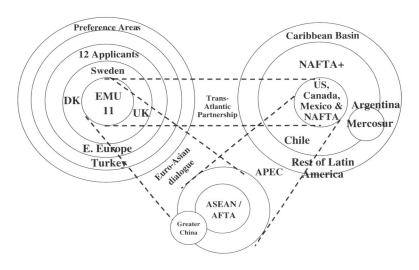

Source: Author.

trade alone accounts for 22 per cent of world trade, and which, overall, accounts for 35 per cent. The EU's trade relationships can be seen in terms of a hierarchy of preferential associations – though some of these are non-reciprocal and are therefore not 'club' agreements in the sense described above.

The institutional arrangements behind the three regional structures are, however, quite different. The EU is (now) a single, common market with ambitions to 'ever closer union' including political, defence and full economic union. NAFTA is a free trade area albeit with limited regulatory convergence (over environment and labour practices). The East Asian region has no formal structure outside ASEAN and the Australia–New Zealand Closer Economic Relations Trade Agreement, but the region has in effect produced a form of non-exclusive 'open regionalism' based on direct investment flows (and also linked by the networks of the Chinese trading community).

One crucial issue is whether or not regional clubs are broadly consistent with wider global liberalization (Bhagwati, 1993; Blackhurst and Henderson, 1993; Cable and Henderson, 1994). The answer is likely to be ambiguous in trade terms since basic customs union theory suggests an indeterminate mix of trade creation and trade diversion (even within free trade areas without a common external tariff). The case for believing that regional clubs reinforce global integration is underpinned by past experience. Empirical work suggests that trade creation has greatly outweighed trade diversion within the EU, except in agriculture (Winters, 1987). The EU has not retreated, as pessimists feared, into a 'fortress': it supported the conclusion of the Uruguay Round and subsequent strengthening of the multilateral system, and there has been a steady process of enlargement, diluting exclusivity. Regional agreements have pioneered new approaches to deeper integration which have had wider application: liberalization of services within the EU, and acceptance of 'mutual recognition' as a principle for product standards to deepen the Single Market.

To set against this generally positive story is a more negative case: that regional clubs work against stronger global governance. The EU came close to destroying the Uruguay Round – even though it eventually accepted a deal close to its own demands limiting the extent of liberalization in agriculture. Regional agreements have pioneered potentially damaging innovations from a free trade standpoint (the social and environmental agreements in NAFTA could legitimize the idea – fiercely opposed by poor countries – that low standards arising from poverty are inadmissible). Some protectionist, discriminatory or trade-diverting devices have also been strengthened by regional groups, as with the EU's anti-dumping policy, or NAFTA's 'rules of origin' which restrict cross-border assembly operations. Less definably, but perhaps more importantly, regionalism has diverted time and energy from advancing global liberalization. There is now a recognition that regional agreements need to be monitored and subjected to tighter WTO disciplines than in the past.

(C) Functional clubs
Clubs of governments have long cooperated to manage specific networks, or to set technical and product standards. The medium has been intergovernmental bodies such as the International Telecoms and Postal Unions, the International Maritime Organization and the World Meteorological Office. These intergovernmental organizations have operated as clubs to provide public goods: telecom interoperability; agreements between countries to deliver each other's mail; international weather monitoring and forecasts; agreed seas lanes and common understanding of ship safety – the plimsoll line, for example; communication between air traffic controllers and common aviation signs and language.

What is changing is the rapid growth in the extent of international integration and in the scale of externalities requiring management. The traditional intergovernmental processes have been struggling to keep up. There has been a parallel change in many countries to denationalize state institutions through privatization and towards systems of regulation based on rules and the enforcement of competition rather than detailed intervention. The functional clubs which have emerged are, in response, eclectic and informal, usually mixtures of state- and private-sector, technical and political interests. Two of the best examples are the financial sector and telecoms, which are reviewed in technical detail in an appendix to this chapter.

The limits of self-regulating globalization

The appendix below describes two specific sector examples which illustrate the way in which decentralized and informal, specialized, networks of regulators (and self-regulators) and standard-setters have had to emerge to meet the challenges of globalization. These operate in quite different ways from the old hierarchical, bureaucratic structures still to be found in some international public-sector organizations. But they are effective in the technically complex and low-profile world of standard-setting.

Within the limited constraints of self-regulation, the globalization process has been market-driven. Private firms have been its motor. It has proceeded hand in hand with the liberalization and deregulation of economies and the withdrawal of the role of the state. Globalization has not automatically led to an enhanced role for the international public sector. The role of the UN in the economic field is negligible. Its main deliberative body, ECOSOC, is unknown to all except a few junior diplomats who attend it. An agency such as UNIDO, which 20 years ago aspired to allocate industrial activity between countries, struggles to avoid closure and to find something to do, like a Soviet-era heavy manufacturing plant in the new Russia. The role of even the more market-friendly institutions that are strongly supported by Western governments, such as the World Bank and IMF, is much diminished from that envisaged earlier in their history.

International economic integration has proceeded apace, albeit unevenly and with structures of governance which are often improvised and underdeveloped. Some of the inadequacies of this system are now becoming apparent and are reviewed in the next chapter.

Appendix: Functional clubs

(A) Global financial markets and standard-setting

Functional clubs have come into existence to address the different ways in which the spread of financial services across borders generates externalities or spillovers beyond those captured in domestic systems of regulation (O'Brien, 1992). There are several such externalities, some widely accepted and others very controversial:

- the benefits from cross-border competition and the desirability, therefore, of regimes that encourage national authorities to open up their financial markets to foreign competition.
- the benefits of common or compatible, 'interoperable', standards – in accounting and audit, for example – which enable financial institutions to function efficiently across borders.
- cross-border externalities in the form of efficient clearance and settlement procedures between institutions of different origin operating in different markets.
- risks, in the absence of prudential, minimum safety standards, of the collapse of a financial institution in a loosely regulated market with low capital adequacy requirements creating a financial crisis among overseas institutions with which it has links. There are, however, those who would argue that stringent prudential conditions can impose unnecessary costs on bank customers and encourage bad habits which would be better curbed by experience of market disciplines; they would question the magnitude of negative externalities (and suspect that, often, standards are used as a market access barrier). This debate has been at the root of different approaches to the recent financial crisis in Asia.
- risks of a weakening of consumer protection if, for example, overseas banks or securities houses offer a service more prone to fraud than domestic operators. It is, however, not clear that these problems represent a market failure calling for international cooperation over regulation rather than a failure by investors to make sensible decisions on their own.
- dangers, in unregulated markets, of money-laundering, helping criminals to obtain financial sanctuary in weak jurisdictions, protected by secrecy or undemanding tests of financial probity. While the Commonwealth club is currently trying to establish rules

of good practice and there are partially successful efforts to oblige Swiss banks to yield up their secrets (typically the details of accounts held by Nazi-era officials holding stolen Jewish assets; or the fortunes of former dictators such as Ferdinand Marcos), it is not clear that the characteristics of markets which make money-laundering possible, notably absolute confidentiality for individual accounts, are intrinsically bad.

While there are theoretical and practical debates about which externalities do call for international regulation, most of the above are now the subject of growing cooperative endeavour. In banking, the first major stage in building a global regulatory regime was the Concordat of the Basle Committee on Banking Regulation and Supervisory Practices made up of G10 (now 11) central bank governors with its secretariat at the Bank for International Settlements (O'Brien, 1992; Steil, 1996; Helleiner, 1994). The Bank is still dominated by rich countries but it has admitted, on a restricted basis, Brazil, China, India and Saudi Arabia. Successive revisions in response to financial scandals and incipient financial crises affecting a series of banks – Herstatt; Banco Ambrosiano, the Bank of Credit and Commerce International – have gradually shifted the locus of responsibility away from the home country towards host country supervision and have engendered closer coordination between the two (Underhill, 1996).

A second major step has been the establishment of capital adequacy accords, first agreed in 1998, designed to prevent competition between markets in the form of tolerance of imprudent levels of capitalization by banks. In particular, banking systems with lower capital adequacy standards (such as Japan's) were required to finance costly capital replenishment. These standards, and more general principles of banking supervision, have now been widely adopted within the BIS 'club' without treaty sanctions.

The process of achieving agreement between regulators in different types of financial markets constantly struggles to keep pace with market developments including 'regulatory risk arbitrage' (whereby banks with a greater appetite for risk have used new financial instruments to assume greater risk while observing the formal capital adequacy criteria). A flexible, largely voluntary system of regulation has been seen, so far, as the only one which could possibly succeed in such a fluid environment in which new technical challenges are constantly emerging. For example, banks have agreed a code of disclosure of their derivatives exposure. The

BIS Committee on Payment and Settlement Systems has produced arrangements to manage settlement risk. Whatever its achievements, however, the system of regulatory cooperation manifestly failed to signal, and stop, the damaging burst of imprudent lending to East Asia. The way in which this global regime operates is through a flexible and rather exclusive committee structure where authority no longer derives exclusively, or even mainly, from governments. Many central bank governors who are represented on the committee are constitutionally independent (Germany, US, France, now the UK). The issues involved in international banking are, moreover, highly esoteric and the global regulatory regime largely reflects a consensus among independent, expert, regulators and the regulated private sector. Governments, let alone parliaments, rarely intrude (Underhill, 1996; Coleman and Porter, 1994).

The process of regulatory divorce from government is carried one step further by IOSCO – the International Organization of Securities Commissions, based in Montreal – which explicitly describes itself as a non-governmental organization. Its members are official national securities regulators such as the US Securities and Exchange Commission (SEC), but the organization functions with the active participation of 'affiliates' (self-regulatory organizations, trade associations or member firms). Much of its operational work – including the harmonization of accounting standards, or policy development on clearance and settlement issues – is the responsibility of industry professionals such as accountants' professional bodies, or independent think-tanks (the G30), or self-selecting groups based on the most advanced financial markets (the Technical Committee on International Transactions).

This largely self-regulating structure has led to the emergence of global capital adequacy standards appropriate to the particular, but fluid, characteristics of the securities industry and designed to reduce regulatory arbitrage. The complexities of the issues, such as the use of mathematically advanced portfolio models to define capital and risk, have been complicated by the overlap between banking and securities markets and by parallel negotiations over standards within the EU which was attempting to define a capital adequacy standard for the Single Market. The fundamental issue at stake in negotiations has been the tension between market competition and uniform minimum standards. The US SEC has been leading the move for high standards of capital adequacy (arguing the case on prudential grounds but suspected by competitor financial markets – the EU and Japan – of seeking to impose costs on them). The issues are not fully resolved but there is now an acceptance of the principle of minimum standards.

All of this activity has produced a convergence of approaches to prudential regulation using the functional 'clubs' of BIS and IOSCO. But the difficulties in making progress are also illustrated in relation to a more prosaic subject: different reporting and accounting standards. At present, under national standards, it is possible for a company to show profits in one jurisdiction and losses in another based on the same data. In a world of cross-listings and global capital markets such idiosyncrasies, so confusing to investors, are inefficient and give rise to real economic costs. A committee of accountants' representatives has been working for over 20 years to develop common standards.

Disagreements remain, however, over whether agreed global standards should replace national standards, be provided in parallel for multinational companies or be reconciled with national standards through harmonization (the European Union has dropped ideas for an additional tier of European standards). There is an evolving system of international standards (IAS) but also resistance to overriding the idiosyncrasies of national systems. In particular, the US SEC questions the quality of international standards in relation to investor protection while US accounting principles (GAAP) are seen as an obstacle to overseas companies seeking a US listing. Canada and Japan have also resisted global standards. An unlikely coalition of EU, Chinese and Arab accountants is leading the move for a new global order. Harmonization is probably too complex to achieve this objective quickly. So a weaker solution has emerged with internationally endorsed, core, standards forming the accounting basis for 3–4,000 global companies and becoming accepted in a growing number of countries, but with continued national reporting where required. Thus a modest, voluntary, *à la carte* approach has evolved to create a set of rules for one of the key components of the globalized economy. An agreement in 1998 – at a meeting of 16 members of the International Accounting Standards Committee, drawn from the accountancy profession world-wide – is something of a triumph for this style of international rule-making.

But the domino-like collapse of financial markets in 1998 also suggests that while the informal style of cooperation on financial regulation and standard-setting has achieved much, it is too weak to cope with systemic collapse.

(B) Telecoms and information standard-setting

As with financial services, there is a set of cross-border externalities which arise when a previously national, and nationally regulated, industry is subject to global integration:

- *interoperability benefits.* Put at its simplest, international calls cannot be made (or networks used for cross-border traffic, e.g. the Internet) unless different national systems can physically connect. Efficient interconnection also generates economies of scale. There are several specific standards problems where these benefits can be realized: common number codes; common reference and measurement standards (such as metrication and use of some waveband conventions); physical interconnection between different national operators; and standard interfaces so that compatible equipment or software can be deployed (for receivers and transmitters of telephony, for example).
- *network externalities.* In addition to externalities arising from physical interconnection, there are benefits from an agreed clearance system for financial settlement (which in telecoms involves prior agreement on the price of incoming and outgoing calls).
- *competition benefits.* The benefits of competition in telecoms have only recently and partially been acknowledged, and liberalization is restricted to a few countries. The idea that there are additional benefits to forcing national operators to compete with foreign operators on an equal basis is even newer and more restricted in application but is now subject to liberalization agreements within the WTO and at regional level.
- in some specific cases – the allocation of spectrum for satellite transmission – there is an *international common good* which calls for a cooperative approach to management.
- *negative spillover effects* may arise from deregulation – e.g. pornography on international telephone services.

Recognition of the need for interoperability standards goes back well over a century in this industry, which was one of the first to establish an intergovernmental organization (the ITU, in 1865) for the general purpose of facilitating international telegraphy (David and Schurmer, 1996). In 1906 an international committee was established specifically in order to advance standards for electrical equipment. Another element in

Figure 3.4: World governance (2)

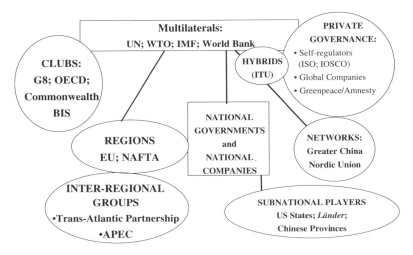

CLUBS:
G8; OECD;
Commonwealth
BIS

REGIONS
EU; NAFTA

INTER-REGIONAL
GROUPS
•Trans-Atlantic Partnership
•APEC

Multilaterals:
UN; WTO; IMF; World Bank

HYBRIDS
(ITU)

NATIONAL
GOVERNMENTS
and
NATIONAL.
COMPANIES

PRIVATE
GOVERNANCE:
• Self-regulators
(ISO; IOSCO)
• Global Companies
• Greenpeace/Amnesty

NETWORKS:
Greater China
Nordic Union

SUBNATIONAL PLAYERS
US States; *Länder*;
Chinese Provinces

Source: Author.

the international regulatory structure, specifically concerned with standard-setting, was the International Organization for Standardization, a non-government body established in 1947 which deals with standards outside telecommunications narrowly defined (reserved to the ITU) and the electro-technical (IEC). In practice a complex structure has emerged involving these three bodies, with overlapping committees (the IEC and ISO deal with information technology), national affiliates of the global bodies – government and non-governmental – and a group of regional standards bodies (Figure 3.4) (David, 1987; Cowhey and Aronson, 1993).

One of the central characteristics of the international standards-setting process is that it has largely been driven by 'technocratic idealism' (David and Schurmer, 1996). It has created a largely non-political culture, cutting across the boundaries of the public and private sector, and based on some general principles: consensus-building, usually involving unanimity; transparency; open, non-discriminatory, participation; due process; and voluntary adoption (except for some safety and quality standards where compliance is obligatory). More than a thousand standards a year are agreed in this way.

The intensification of global integration has, however, put the system under considerable strain. There are two main problems. First, the consensus-building processes are slow in an environment where techno-logical change and innovation are very fast. It can typically take seven years to obtain an international standard, and much longer for contro-versial ones (e.g. electric sockets). This leads to the process being bypassed, and standards being developed commercially. Microsoft's MS-DOS, for example, crucial to the development of information technology, is not a 'free' international standard but a proprietorial one which has come to dominate through commercial competition. Welfare losses as a result of a monopolistic private standard have to be set alongside the benefits in terms of economies of scale and scope from having a global standard on the market quickly. Economic analysis is ambiguous about the relative merits of formal standard-setting, involving consensus among a multiplicity of players, and market-based alternatives (David and Monroe, 1994).

A second problem is that standards can be used for mercantilist purposes. Idiosyncratic standards can be used to protect national (or regional) industries from overseas competition. Alternatively, the develop-ment of strong national standards, associated with distinctive quality, can be a means to promote exports and to obtain 'strategic' advantage in terms of higher prices. The history of fragmented colour television standards (leading to the development of three incompatible standards) was a classic example of this approach and was repeated with high definition TV. There is a danger of some debilitating conflict over digital mobile telephony. A global standard (GSM) originated in Europe and has been adopted in 105 countries. But, in the US, separate systems are being developed by AT&T (TDMS) and Qualcom (CDMA). The growing importance of regional standards has sometimes been seen as a mechan-ism for translating mercantilism into the context of regional 'blocs' with different, rival, incompatible and potentially protectionist standards. Certainly there has been an enormous burst of regional standard-setting in Europe in bodies such as ETSI and CENELEC. Although it is difficult to see much evidence of a 'fortress Europe' developing through telecoms or other standards at present, the potential exists for friction between different regional styles and procedures for standard-setting.

The stresses and strains on formal standard-setting processes, especi-ally those which have relied on government-to-government relationships, are being further aggravated by deregulation and liberalization. National carriers are launching into cross-industry and cross-border alliances and coalitions (see Figure 3.5). The boundaries of 'industries' are becoming blurred, creating turf disputes and clashes of styles (the IT sector operating

Figure 3.5: Telecoms corporate alliances

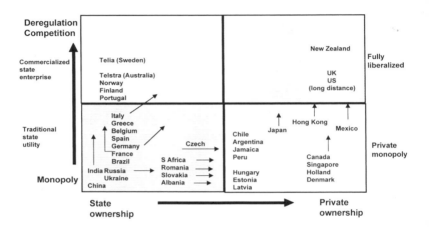

Source: Cable and Distler, 1995.

mainly with proprietary standards or private consortia; telecoms mainly with regulated, consensus-based, standards).

What is emerging is a more flexible form of governance with hybridized public/private-sector standard-setting (the ITU now admits private companies) and a greater willingness to pool national sovereignty in the interests of achieving rapid standard-setting. ISO, ITU, IEC, CEN, CENELEC all now employ qualified majority voting – with ETSI in North America allowing the refinement of weighted voting to reflect the relative size of national telecoms companies.

A potentially radical change to the international standard-setting process is presented by the concept of the 'global information infra-structure' (GII) which has been defined to include the widespread use of broadband services delivering multimedia and other new services; a further development of inter-networked data communications beyond those offered by the Internet; and the creation of easy access to permit effective competition in all aspects of telecommunications. GII is some-times called the 'global superhighway' idea (David and Steinmueller,

1996). The GII vision involves a conceptual leap from the existing standards structures which are still largely rooted in national organizations, with limited bilateral and multilateral cooperation. There are different views on how it might be realized. One is to build on the Internet, which has elements of all three central features of the GII (it is capable of supporting broadband, is already pioneering global networking, and creates easy access for new competitors). The decentralized, 'bottom up', approach of the Internet allows for maximum experimentation. Critics argue, however, that the Internet faces serious congestion problems, aggravated by the lack of any mechanism for charging for the marginal cost of using the system (which cannot be rectified on technically available standards). Either the system will suffer severe quality decline or payment will be needed to subsidize the 'network backbone'. These problems suggest that the global 'superhighway' may instead eventually emerge as a result of integrating different national and commercial broadband systems, involving commercial charging for services. In that case, complex standards issues will need to be resolved in order to ensure interoperability and easy network access for competitors. Many of the dilemmas involved in global standard-setting will re-emerge but involve much greater technical complexity, inter-industry linkages and faster speed of decision. It is not yet clear whether informal cooperation between national regulators and commercial interests will suffice to meet these requirements.

Chapter 4

A regulatory deficit

This chapter addresses the deficiencies of a largely informal, improvised, system of economic governance that has grown up to manage globalization. The main concern is with the under-provision of international public goods or regulatory deficiencies at a global level. The most topical relates to systemic risk in financial markets and the first section of the chapter discusses the deficiencies in this area. There have, by contrast, been major advances in creating regulatory structures at regional and global level for facilitating international competition, though rules and standards have lagged some way behind technology and markets. This concern is addressed in the second section.

Systemic risk and financial stability

One of the major questions generated by the emerging market financial crises of 1998 is whether there is adequate provision to deal with systemic risk at a global level.

The vulnerability of financial markets to 'boom and bust' is one of the recurring themes of economic history. And banking crises in particular, originating in widespread default, have occurred with considerable frequency. The last two decades have included the developing-country – mostly Latin American – debt crisis of the 1980s; the equity markets crash of 1987; the savings and loan débâcle in the US; the pricking of the Japanese asset bubble and its effects on financial intermediaries; and a banking crisis in Scandinavia in the early 1990s: all before the 1998 crisis erupted in Thailand and spread through East Asia. It is tempting to conclude that since all these recent crises have been managed without serious damage to the world economy as a whole (albeit with serious costs to some countries and many individuals), the system is reasonably robust. Yet there are good reasons for believing that there are great dangers in the current situation and serious deficiencies in the system of governance.

First, the sheer volume and volatility of short-term cross-border capital movements now has the capacity to create major adjustment problems for those countries that have to respond to them. Developing countries – and within that group a small number of countries including Malaysia, South Korea and Thailand – attracted around $200 bn in private funds in both 1995 and 1996, a large proportion in the form of portfolio share investments or short-term loans from banks to private borrowers. These flows became very large in relation to the size of domestic markets or foreign-exchange reserves, increasing the danger that either would be dramatically affected by a change in perception of risk and very large capital outflows. What was destabilizing was the relatively vast pool of highly leveraged capital – hedge funds supported by bank capital – focused specifically on emerging markets and liable to make large rapid portfolio changes in response to margin calls. The current-account adjustment from non-traded activities to traded activities required in response to large capital movements can be immensely difficult. The five most seriously affected counties (South Korea, Indonesia, Malaysia, Thailand and the Philippines) faced a massive, painful, adjustment of around 7 per cent of GDP in 1998 as a result of sudden outflows of $100 bn, in the absence of large external balance-of-payments support. There is a great temptation for governments to disconnect from free capital flows in these circumstances and to pursue more autarkic policies – as Malaysia and also Russia have opted to do.

Second, there is clear evidence of financial contagion such that sudden large capital movements do not derive – or only derive – from the specifics of host country economic performance but involve spillovers from one country to another. The recent academic literature is somewhat ambiguous on this point. Some work suggests that large capital outflows from Mexico and Southeast Asian countries represented a rational response to discounted expected cash flows and risk (Wolf, 1997). Other work suggests that there is a large unexplained, 'irrational' element in the timing of currency crises which can only be attributed to panic or contagion (Eichengreen, Rose and Wyplosz, 1996).

There are several overlapping arguments about international financial contagion. One relates to whether crises are in fact 'contagious' between countries. Another issue is whether investors behave in a 'herd-like' way, aggravating the magnitude of financial crises. A third is whether the behaviour of investors is 'rational' (herd-like behaviour and contagion may be rational but still economically undesirable). A literature has emerged explaining why investors behave in a predictable but herd- like way, leading to systemic problems with banking collapse and wider financial crises in a succession of countries (Devenow and Welch, 1996). The process is explained by imperfect information. Small banks may well rely on large banks to do their homework for them amid ignorance and uncertainty, for example about emerging markets. Managers may gain reputations from being orthodox rather than right. There may well also be self-fulfilling expectations in herd behaviour.

There is another body of literature explaining why crises pass from one country to another; in other words, how contagion spreads. There is the idea of the 'wake up call' as investors are alerted by failures in one country to weaknesses in others (Goldstein, 1995b). (In Asia, the Thai crisis raised awareness of banking weakness elsewhere.) Devaluation in one country is likely to trigger devaluations elsewhere by undermining other countries' competitiveness, and this was certainly a factor in Asia (Glick and Rose, 1999). Direct financial linkages may be important (as between Korean banks and Russian debt).

The combination of these various factors suggests that international capital markets may be very unstable. By their own behaviour they can trigger a collapse of currencies or (if exchange rates are floating) large exchange-rate movements. This can in turn contribute to financial instability in affected countries, to a greater extent than is justified by policy failures in those countries, suggesting that there is a deficiency in arrangements for stopping a market panic impacting on large numbers of countries. This in turn raises the issue as to whether there is need for an international lender of last resort and who should perform that role.

A global lender of last resort?

When a financial crisis occurs in a domestic economy the national Central Bank can, as a last resort, make unlimited liquidity available to collapsing financial institutions to prevent the spread of panic. There is no direct equivalent at an international level to prevent financial contagion. Various options exist or have been canvassed for the international equivalent of a Central Bank lender of last resort function. One approach is to create – or develop within the IMF – a large pool of emergency funds. The current problem with this approach is that the IMF does not have remotely adequate funding to meet a rapid or overlapping series of crises. And its deliberative, conditional lending process is inappropriate to a panic environment where decisions to deploy large amounts of capital have to be taken within hours rather than weeks or months. A substantially enlarged IMF may be desirable in any event to help economies adjust with supporting finance; but the IMF is not designed for crises of financial contagion. There are, however, other options. Under provisions such as the General Agreement to Borrow, leading Western countries can mobilize substantial sums from financial markets in an emergency, using their own creditworthiness, to lend quickly at market rates and with minimal conditionality to countries stricken by a collapse of external confidence.

Resistance to providing this support reflects concern over the 'moral hazard' problem. Put simply, imprudent commercial lenders should not be protected from their folly, otherwise they will simply repeat it. And governments which accommodate imprudent borrowing by their nationals (or are financially imprudent themselves) will, similarly, perpetuate profligate behaviour. The argument is based on the fact that banking (like some other forms of financial intermediation) is inherently risky, with a slender base of reserves supporting a large column of assets. Unless rewards and penalties reflect performance in risk management, financial markets will not work; successful banks will be those with a talent for lobbying politicians and regulators to bail them out. Those concerns are germane to the recent crisis since – arguably – experience of the rescue operation for Mexico in 1994/5 was one factor in reducing perception of risk in emerging markets, particularly Russia. While investors almost certainly did not put money into East Asia expecting to be bailed out, it could reasonably be argued that they were very foolish and that, had they been more conscious of risk, they would have realized that a long history of highly protected banking in East Asia had led to the creation of financial institutions which were in no fit state to withstand the impact of capital liberalization.

Preoccupation with moral hazard would, however, lead to the conclusion that no action is required to effect any rescue involving collapsing financial institutions (beyond existing national deposit insurance). Any foreign bank which underestimated currency and transfer risk in lending to Asia (as well as normal commercial risk associated with lending) could have no complaint and expect no redress from its home country government if the borrower defaulted or the borrower country blocked debt service.

In practice, the idea that the recent financial crisis in Asia and Latin America owed much to moral hazard is far-fetched. There is no indication that countries have any desire for IMF conditional lending or would court financial disaster knowing the powerful social and political consequences. Nor has there been much of a 'bail out'. Foreign banks have had to set aside funds against losses on their loans to emerging markets and write off debts. Equity investors in emerging markets have lost heavily.

Some countries, moreover, have suffered from financial contagion which had little to do with imprudent policy. In the absence of external financial support, there has also been a real risk that governments would not accept the painful consequences of a loss of confidence and resort to capital and trade controls. Or they might – as both Brazil and Russia have done – accept a move to a floating exchange rate but at a cost that includes a reduced ability to lower inflation expectations. Moral hazard may be a real problem but not necessarily an overriding concern. Indeed, in a major crisis, more damage may be inflicted through inaction stemming from concern about moral hazard than through a concerted rescue operation. To the extent that moral hazard is a problem in big rescue operations it can be reduced by agreed debt reduction where creditors carry a significant share of the burden; and can be minimized by the use of privately negotiated credit lines (as for Argentina) rather than taxpayers' money.

There are other ways in which governments of major economies can perform a 'lender of last resort' function within the international system. One is to provide sufficient liquidity to head off recession induced by a general crisis of confidence The reaction of the Federal Reserve and other authorities acting in concert in 1987 was widely credited with averting a serious recession (though at the cost of stimulating inflation). The concerted round of interest-rate cuts in 1998, and in particular the uninterrupted economic expansion of the US, has been sufficient to provide a 'consumer of last resort', thereby sustaining economic growth in the face of weak confidence levels.

The immediate concerns, however, are the deficiency of arrangements for stopping a market panic from impacting on large numbers of countries, and more specifically whether the IMF adequately performs the role of emergency lender to head off contagious crises.

The IMF as a last resort lender

The recent crises in Asia, Russia and Brazil have led to serious criticism of the IMF and to a wider re-examination of its role. First, as already noted, those who are concerned about moral hazard have attacked it for blunting the sense of risk to banks, and encouraging imprudent lending. The IMF saw the issue as a trade-off:

> Faced with a crisis, we could allow it to deepen and possibly teach international lenders a lesson in the process; alternatively, we can step in to do what we can to mitigate effects of the crisis to the region and the world economy in a way that places some of the burden on borrowers and lenders, although possibly with some undesirable side effects. (Fischer, 1998)

Second, and more seriously, several key programmes failed in their objective to maintain external confidence, notably in Russia and more recently in Brazil. The counter to this is that there have been successes as well as failures. In 1994/95, intervention in Mexico prevented a financial crisis which could have spilled over to other countries, leading to exchange controls, debt default and disruptions of private capital flows to developing countries. Although the IMF was made to look foolish in Korea after producing a glowing report on the country's macroeconomic situation a few weeks before the crisis, the recent programmes in Korea and Thailand have already led to a resumption of growth and have prompted far-reaching financial sector reform. The attempts to rein in fiscal imbalances in Brazil were not abandoned in the wake of the January 1999 currency crisis and devaluation. The only total failure has been Russia, but that reflects not only deep domestic policy problems, notably in fiscal policy, but also external factors such as the weakened oil price.

Third, the price of IMF support in the form of conditionality incorporating rapid, severe, fiscal consolidation and big interest-rate increases has also seemed disproportionate to any policy failures and politically difficult to deliver, tempting countries such as Malaysia down the path of alternative strategies. There is a vast literature on the experience of adjustment in developing and transition economies (Killick, 1983) but the complex issues involved usually boil down to identifying a counter, factual case: what would be the alternative to an IMF programme? The current discussion of alternatives revolves largely around the question of whether it would have been possible to stabilize collapsing currencies by means other than temporary large increases in interest rates (which have deflated demand and precipitated solvency crises among domestic borrowers). The alternative of temporary capital controls has been canvassed, as in Malaysia. But it is far from clear that the Malaysian 'alternative' actually worked; interest rates fell in Korea and Thailand to below Malaysian levels after they pursued more orthodox adjustment and in autumn 1998 there was a serious loss of international confidence in Malaysian securities in overseas markets at a time when Korea and Thailand were re-emerging as international borrowers. But, since Malaysia is also now recovering, those who forecast dire consequences from heterodox solutions have also been confounded

More fundamentally, the alternative of 'financing rather than adjustment' or slower adjustment with the help of external finance depends on the finance available. The total capital base of the IMF after recent increases in quotas is currently around $284 bn, excluding $45 bn available under the new Agreement to Borrow. Although the sums are large, the amounts available for deployment in an emergency are much smaller. And total resources are less than a third of the daily turnover of leading foreign exchange markets and around 5 per cent of annual world trade. The IMF is now a third as big in relation to world output as it was in 1945. There is a resource constraint which limits its capacity to be a lender of last resort, especially of several countries at once. It could be argued that the resources required would be much smaller if there were less attachment to fixed exchange rates. While the proposition may well be true to a degree, it is optimistic to imagine that a generalized shift to floating rates will increase financial stability overall. Among transition economies and other countries with an experience of high inflation, inflation has been more effectively cured by fixed rates, as has happened in Argentina, Brazil (until the real crisis in 1999), Poland in 1990–91, Estonia, the Czech and Slovak Republics, Croatia (Banarjee et al., 1995; Calvo et al., 1993; Sahay and Vegh, 1995).

With the benefit of hindsight, Western governments have acknowledged that the IMF was under-funded to perform the roles demanded of it in a crisis of contagion. It is already moving to establish a 'lender of last resort role' through a 'supplementary reserve facility' to make short-term loans at penalty rates of interest, and is also establishing a precautionary facility for countries which pre-qualify. The hard-won negotiations to provide $18 bn from the US Congress will strengthen the Fund's ability to perform this role. Moreover there is now a broad recognition that international capital markets are not working as well as good domestic markets; that the onus for adjusting to market failures cannot be placed disproportionately on borrowers from developing and transition countries; and that the IMF should assume a much more explicit role as lender of last resort than in the past (Fischer, 1998). The main criticism which can now be made is that the response has been too little, too late.

International financial supervision

One of the main lessons of the succession of financial crises in 1997 and 1998 has been that a combination of weak banking systems and freedom of capital movements is a very dangerous mix. Most attempts, by the IMF in particular, to designate appropriate conditions for capital liberalization have emphasized macroeconomic policy rather than the reform of financial-sector institutions and regulation. Indeed, prudent monetary and fiscal policies combined with liberalization have encouraged excessive flows from the standpoint of the capacity of the emerging market banking systems.

Weakly supervised and badly managed banks have helped to convert a problem into a crisis in several ways (Greenspan, 1998). They obtained considerable volumes of funding from overseas when interest-rate conditions were favourable, exposing them to a risk of collapse in different circumstances. In some cases there was an implicit assumption that governments would rescue any banks which got into trouble because of the authorities' failure to distinguish between emergency liquidity support in a crisis and blanket guarantees to protect banks which became insolvent because of poor practices.

As described in the previous chapter, responsibility for ensuring good practice and establishing international standards has fallen to the Basle-based Bank for International Settlements through its Committee of Banking Supervisors (and IOSCO for securities markets). The Basle Committee has established some core principles for effective bank supervision and its capital adequacy rules for safer banking have been widely adopted (Folkerts-Landau and Lindgren, 1998). The negotiation of these common standards was, however, achieved only after considerable delay and difficulty because of suspicions that countries with low capital adequacy standards (e.g. Japan) were seeking to achieve competitive advantage by lowering the cost of capital.

Following the succession of financial disasters in recent years it is reasonable to ask whether the existing international arrangements have failed and should be replaced by a single 'super regulator' for financial markets incorporating the IMF and the BIS. Criticisms of the BIS system (described in more detail in Chapter 3) centre on several points. First, the system has mostly involved developed countries, though a few major emerging-market Central Bank supervisors have been included in recent years. Second, the capital standards set for banks have not kept up with the range of hazards involved in international finance (e.g. not just making imprudent investments but raising capital in excessively risky ways by borrowing abroad on the assumption of a stable exchange-rate peg).

However, the problems in this area are not of a kind that can easily be solved by shifting the institutional goal posts. Prudential regulation is not easy. Supervisors need to be highly skilled in increasingly complex and sophisticated banking activities where – for example – complex mathematical modelling is used for part of this management. The issue is not just one of technical expertise but of political independence and an ability to withstand political pressures. Attempts to minimize difficulties by setting simple rules may be counterproductive, as with Thai regulations to limit foreign exposure by banks which led to their passing exposure to domestic customers.

Within these constraints, various proposals have been made drawing on the lessons of the Asian crisis (Mathiesson, Richards and Sharma, 1998). One is to recalibrate the BIS capital adequacy rules to give greater weighting to risk and to short-term loans. A second relates to the need to offset the destabilizing effect of short-term, cross-border, inter-bank lending where risk is blurred by official promises of guarantees, such as were offered recently in Korea, Indonesia and Thailand. Greenspan (1998) has suggested financial penalties through fees or more stringent capital adequacy requirements. Third, unconventional supervisory measures could be encouraged for emerging markets – such as restricting foreign borrowing and limiting domestic lender of last resort responsibilities to a narrow range of banks. Fourth, there is a general predisposition towards greater transparency in the financial sector, through disclosure requirements (though transparency is often recited as a mantra and ignores the real practical problem that when transparency reveals failings it may trigger a stampede). Last, banks cannot be reformed in isolation from the corporate sector which is their major customer. A particular problem area is the absence of satisfactory bankruptcy law, without which periods of financial crisis are compounded by a panic 'grab race' among creditors, including bankers, thereby aggravating crisis conditions (La Porta and Lopez de Silanes, 1998). Better bankruptcy proceedings require stronger, internationally comparable, auditing and accounting standards which are being generated by the Committee on Accounting Standards, described in the appendix to Chapter 3.

In short, there are several steps which can be taken, at an international level, to strengthen the supervision and regulation of financial markets, so providing an important public good in a globalizing economy. One major unresolved issue, however, is whether free capital flows should be restricted until more effective financial supervision can be established.

Capital controls

In addition to measures to rescue countries from crisis there is the question of how future crises are to be prevented. There has been a revival of interest in measures to stem capital flows. One approach to try to reduce financial instability is by slowing or stopping short-term capital movements. Temporary capital controls have recently attracted theoretical support (Bhagwati, 1998; Rodrick, 1998; Wolf, 1997). Their main application is in an environment where governments are trying to cut interest rates to head off deflation but are simultaneously trying to prevent a collapse of the currency as capital flows out in search of higher returns elsewhere. It is not yet clear whether the reintroduction of capital controls in Malaysia – and their strengthening in China – will work (because of the scope for evasion) and whether they will be temporary or become permanent. A sensible, pragmatic, approach is not to treat such controls as an issue of dogma – one way or the other – but to ensure that they are carefully monitored and dismantled as the crisis eases.

Another, less controversial, version of capital controls is to dampen down volatile capital movements by restricting inflows through taxes (as in Chile) or taxing short-term capital transactions in general (the so-called 'Tobin Tax', after the Nobel Laureate James Tobin). Both of these ideas work with the grain of the market and both are consistent with open economies. The Tobin Tax has been widely applauded as a concept, but there is little sign of success in finding ways to overcome the formidable technical problems of tracing numerous electronic exchange transactions in order to tax them. The proliferation of derivatives would also make the tax base very difficult to identify. National schemes may be easier to operate. The Chile model – now being phased out – has appeared to work reasonably well and may be of wider interest to countries with underdeveloped domestic financial markets which might attract and be destabilized by sudden capital inflows (followed by sudden outflows).

It is now widely acknowledged that opening up semi-reformed, underdeveloped financial markets to the demands of full capital convertibility is not appropriate. It is noteworthy, however, that Germany and Switzerland which had systems analogous to Chile's, and indeed Chile itself, have abandoned controls as impractical.

Exchange rates, the IMF and international coordination
The inevitability of capital mobility and the limited scope for capital controls have undermined the ability of governments to maintain fixed, nominal, exchange rates. So much was evident in major economies at the time of the end of the Bretton Woods system in 1973. One of the lessons of the Asian crisis is that, even with the support of the IMF and with broadly prudent macroeconomic policies, it has not been possible to peg nominal exchange rates in the face of strong speculative pressure. All the crisis-hit Asian economies, as well as Russia and Brazil, were trying to maintain fixed pegs.

Globalization of financial markets imposes stark choices on governments. One option is to allow the exchange rate to float freely as it does for major economies such as those of the US, Japan, Germany (now the euro) and Canada. The theoretical arguments for floating rates are long established (Friedman, 1953). In practice businesses learn the necessity for hedging and thereby insure against instability, at a price. But, especially for smaller, more open, economies there is a risk of instability as volatile capital flows lead to serious 'overshooting'. Consequently managed floating – with central banks using interest rates to control exchange-rate movements – as opposed to completely free floating remains popular (India, Croatia, Czech Republic, Turkey, Egypt), as does a variant, the crawling peg (Hungary, Poland, Israel), whereby devaluation takes place on a controlled, staged basis. Some of the more successful exchange-rate policies in recent years have involved the use of a fixed rate to act as a brake on inflation followed by controlled devaluation to maintain export competitiveness (as in Poland and Israel). But in a world of free capital movements such control is difficult to maintain unless short-term interest rates are used primarily for exchange-rate management rather than for managing domestic demand.

If the alternative of a fixed exchange rate is sought, the requirements are now more demanding than was the case before the 1998 crisis exposed the frailty of currency pegs (Eichengreen, 1995). One option is a currency board under which domestic monetary policy responds to changes in the foreign-exchange position and, thus, to the balance of capital flows as well as trade, much as occurred under the gold standard or with colonial currency boards. Although this approach has been advocated for Indonesia and Brazil the political disciplines required have been seen (quite reasonably) as implausibly severe. This regime seems likely to work only for small countries (such as the Baltics in relation to the euro or some Latin American countries in relation to the dollar) where the authorities are willing to surrender monetary sovereignty to secure financial stability. Sovereignty pooling via a currency union is another option, as in EMU. The disciplines required of members of the embryonic union and market confidence that union would be achieved were remarkably successful in shielding the 11 members of EMU from any speculative attack in 1998 in the build-up to the locking of rates. Market expectations of inflation have been reduced to very low levels even in countries with historically weak financial disciplines. The conditions required for a successful economic and monetary union in Europe are nonetheless demanding and it is not yet altogether clear that they will be met (Begg et al., 1993). It is unlikely that other regimes even further removed from the conditions of an optimum currency area – including a high degree of overlapping trade; factor mobility within the union; and fiscal transfers – will be able to take the EMU route (Mundell, 1961). Nor is there, elsewhere, the same degree of political commitment to regional integration or to building new structures to support it.

Since only a limited number of countries can plausibly achieve completely fixed regimes and since completely floating rates can experience wide variations there is a continuing interest in intermediate solutions. There has been a revival of interest in greater economic coordination including exchange-rate management as between Euroland, Japan and the US (Williamson, 1995; Bergsten and Williamson, 1994; Mundell, 1961; McKinnon, 1988). As in a monetary union, policy coordination reduces the 'spillover' of policy from one country to another (Currie and Whitely, 1993) and the risk of major misalignments. Greater exchange-rate stability could send clearer price signals, facilitating closer trade and investment flows.

In the short term the three main sets of monetary authorities oppose surrendering monetary independence to make a target zone system work, given the limited overlap of economic activity and the very different economic conditions, especially between the US and Japan. But globalization will increase policy spillovers, and a variety of mechanisms have been proposed whereby the IMF could, initially at least, oversee specific concerted actions (Vines, 1997) – as when there is a major misalignment of real exchange rates (Goldstein, 1995a) – or deal with the externalities produced by individual major countries running excessive fiscal deficits (McKinnon, 1988). With closer economic integration, demands to confront these issues will become increasingly insistent.

International debt and bankruptcy

We have already argued that there is an important international public good in a lender of last resort to prevent a liquidity crisis involving 'contagion' spiralling out of control. There is also a case for international action in respect of insolvency: that is, when a crisis results in countries being unable to pay their debt service obligations. In a domestic situation, insolvency leads to a bankruptcy process and – if this is satisfactory – it is possible to make a new start once losses from the debt 'overhang' are distributed among creditors. International lending is different since there is no bankruptcy procedure and there can be a prolonged hiatus between default and creditors agreeing to write off their debts (Portes and Vines, 1996). This hiatus can involve prolonged financial crisis and damage to growth, affecting both creditors and debtor counties.

This problem first arose seriously in the early 1980s with the Latin American debt crisis. By comparison with recent debt crises, that one was relatively simple: the debts were unambiguously those of debtor-country governments or guaranteed by them; most of the debt was accounted for by relatively few creditors – big banks or Western governments; and there was a recognized process – the London and Paris Clubs for bank and official debt respectively – to facilitate debt renegotiation. Nonetheless the episode was far from satisfactory. Latin American growth was interrupted for most of the decade and it took over three years before debt write-offs were agreed under a US government-sponsored initiative. By contrast, the most recent crisis involves debt with an ambiguous status (mostly private but some with implicit government guarantees); there is a more scattered set of creditors (Russian bond holders for example); and because the defaults do not directly threaten the solvency of the Western banking system as happened in the early 1980s there is less pressure to find solutions.

A series of practical reforms has been proposed (Eichengreen and Portes,1995; Miller and Zhang, 1996) to create the international equivalent of smooth domestic bankruptcy proceedings which could well involve the IMF (in, for example, sanctioning delays in repayment). So far, however, this is an area where major, substantive, reform has not yet taken place. But a good deal of practical work is being undertaken by a UN Commission (UNCITRAL) on model bankruptcy laws, the International Bar Association (on a cross-border insolvency concordat) and with the EU – all designed to harmonize and modernize bankruptcy proceedings.

Institutional financial reform and the role of the Bretton Woods institutions

The recent crisis has produced a plethora of proposals for new or reorganized institutions to address some of the deficiencies in the systems of global economic governance identified above:

- A world financial regulator merging the IMF, BIS and World Bank – advocated by the UK government – essentially to create internationally agreed standards of good practice in international finance.
- The IMF as a fully developed international lender of last resort, or the same role performed under different auspices such as the General Agreement to Borrow.
- A global public-sector credit-rating agency in addition to the purely private sector agencies (S&P and Moody's).
- A global central bank as lender of last resort and with greater independence than the IMF to manage global liquidity.
- A global bankruptcy court.
- A debt insurance corporation to counter prolonged loss of creditworthiness.

There seems, however, little merit in creating a batch of new institutions when there is expert knowledge and experience within existing institutions. It is difficult to believe that the IMF and the World Bank together with the plethora of informal international networks could not be adapted to fill the institutional gaps in global economic governance. Nor do mergers have much to commend them unless there is obvious duplication or synergy.

There are essentially three major deficiencies in the current system, highlighted in the recent crisis, which have been described above. The first is the lack of agreed and observed international standards, comparable to standards available in leading domestic markets. These various deficiencies are now being dealt with through cooperative networks of governments, independent regulators and specialist practitioners: financial supervision and regulation through the BIS (banks), IOSCO (securities) and IAIS (insurance); harmonization and improvements in bankruptcy proceedings (UNCITRAL and the International Bar Association); payments systems (the Basle Committee on Settlements); data dissemination designed to improve transparency and accountability (in the IMF, the BIS and the 'Willard Group' of 22 Finance Ministers); greater fiscal transparency (via an IMF code, the OECD and the EMU Stability Pact); improved and compatible auditing and accounting standards (the International Accounting Standards Committee); and corporate governance (the International Corporate Governance Network; OECD; Basle Committee, World Bank). The role of the IMF and, to a lesser extent, the World Bank is to bestow official status on those standards and to help to ensure compliance through their respective roles in conditional lending backed up by research and advice, the IMF predominantly in the field of macroeconomic policy, the Bank in microeconomic development assistance.

Second, there is a genuine global 'lender of last resort' role which the IMF has until now not been able to perform since, as already noted, it has lacked the resources or procedures for rapid, large-scale, lending in an emergency. It is not fundamentally important whether, as is happening, the IMF sprouts new facilities for pre-qualified countries or whether they take place under other existing sets of arrangements (such as the General Agreement to Borrow) or completely new ones.

Third, there has been little macroeconomic policy coordination outside regional groups (EMU) and the broad and loose understandings between G7 finance ministers. Yet as the global economy becomes more interdependent, macroeconomic policy spillovers will increase between major economies. Ironically, the IMF now has virtually no responsibilities in this area although it was heavily involved in its first 25 years of existence in policy coordination – through its oversight of the global fixed exchange-rate system, major exchange-rate adjustments and liquidity provision – when spillovers of policy were less important than today (Vines, 1997; Vines and Stephenson, 1991).

A bigger coordination issue relates to how the economic policies of major countries, both developed and emerging, can' be reconciled with other, wider, global concerns, such as the maintenance of an open trading system or environmental sustainability. The idea of an Economic Security Council – involving leading governments, the WTO, the IMF and the World Bank – is a manifestation of this perceived institutional gap (Carlsson and Ramphal, 1993).

Rules for competition

One of the central challenges facing the global system is creating a common set of rules to govern international competition when there is an enormous range of degrees of international integration by county and sector.

While attempts are being made to create a rules-based structure for relatively new forms of competition – in traded services for example – many old problems remain. Despite decades of trade liberalization within the GATT, there still remain major barriers to trade in goods. Some sectors remain largely untouched by liberalization and are replete with large tariffs and a variety of non-tariff restrictions including quotas. Agriculture and textiles are the two major cases. Although there has been a negotiated agreement to reduce farm subsidies and to phase out textile quotas, the process of dismantling barriers has hardly begun. The WTO is addressing these issues, but only slowly.

The wider policy question concerns how global competition is to be created and regulated across the board. The first-stage problem is creating market access so that providers can enjoy equal – national – treatment in other countries. WTO at a global level, the EU through the Single Market and NAFTA are pushing back the frontiers here. However, in some sectors there has been only a minimal level of agreement to date on the principles which should govern market access. The EU's basic telecommunications liberalization directive, for example, did not take effect until 1998, three years after the WTO agreement on telecommunications, and most market opening that has so far occurred has been the result of unilateral action. There is no agreement yet at a global level on audio-visual services. A WTO agreement on market access for financial services has only been reached with difficulty and the EU single market for financial services is one of the less developed parts of the Union, with protectionist barriers still strong. There is only the outline of an EU 'open skies' policy, and none at a global level beyond limited bilateral (US–UK) understandings. Thus, even in this limited area of creating access for foreign competitors there are large gaps.

The next step is making competition effective once market access has been conceded in principle. It is not always straightforward. The UK has one of the world's most open telecommunications and civil aviation markets but OFTEL continues to struggle to reduce BT's in-built advantages in basic telecoms, while new private airlines find it difficult to break into BA's established routes, especially using Heathrow. There is an embryonic EU competition policy which can be a mechanism for challenging concentrated ownership and anti-competitive behaviour at an EU level, but no comparable global structure to ensure that global markets are made contestable as between the major players. Yet there are many cases in which any meaningful competition policy has to be global: the large airline duopoly of Boeing and Airbus; the telecoms and oil industry alliances being forged; the increasing tendency to airline alliances; the monopoly power carried by Microsoft's software standards; the handful of global news and sports networks; the satellite communications consortia.

A related deficiency is the lack of rules for ensuring that competition not only takes place but does so 'fairly'. This, of course, begs many questions, some of them ethical as well as deriving from competition policy narrowly defined.

What is slowly emerging is a consensus around a set of general principles to govern global competition:

1. Non-discrimination One of the most important, and cherished, principles of the GATT, and now the WTO, is that liberalization benefits which accrue to some members of the international community in terms of market access should apply to all on a non-discriminatory 'Most Favoured Nation' basis.

The non-discriminatory principle has proved difficult to uphold and has been under attack from several directions. First, the principle is counter-intuitive and goes against the mercantilist instinct to restrict 'concessions' to those countries which offer reciprocal benefits. There is, as a result, resentment at *'free riders'* who benefit from global liberalization but make no political sacrifices by liberalizing themselves. Whether the Maldives and Swaziland contribute to trade liberalization is not a significant issue but it has become so for the major industrializing countries of Asia and Latin America. The main concrete manifestations of the issue at present are the demands of the Western countries that China (and Russia) should not enter the WTO as developing countries enjoying non-reciprocal benefits but should make a substantial commitment to liberalization. Another point of conflict is the demand that India, which has hitherto fought a somewhat contradictory campaign – liberalizing its trade regime unilaterally while opposing external disciplines to do the same – should remove trade barriers according to an agreed schedule if it wishes to continue to enjoy benefits. A fiercely contested negotiation has also occurred over financial services, where the US has endeavoured to exclude those Asian countries that had made 'inadequate' offers. Largely thanks to the EU, on this occasion, an agreement on financial services was reached incorporating the non-discriminatory principle. At the time of writing, the non-discriminatory principle is being broadly upheld. But there are those in the West who see

China and Russia as potential enemies and wish to exclude one or both from the multilateral system; and others who see much of the poor world as a disturbing source of competition and wish to draw up discriminatory protective walls against it.

A second – and related – source of attack on non-discrimination has been from those who are impatient with the *slow progress* in achieving consensus among over 150 countries to tackle difficult new issues. The Tokyo Round of negotiations in the 1970s agreed to several 'codes' under which like-minded countries could proceed on a 'conditional Most Favoured Nation' basis. It was expected that the Uruguay Round would follow the same route and, in effect, create a two-tier international system. In the event (and, in retrospect, remarkably) it did not. This was due in large part to the fact that major developing countries including Brazil and India agreed to swallow the (for them) bitter pill of intellectual property protection and liberalizing trade in services.

A third problem is *regionalism*. Common markets and free trade areas are inherently discriminatory. They divert trade as well as create it. The popular psychology supporting regionalism, especially in Europe, has often been defensive, directed against the rest of the world. Neverthless, despite the fashionability of the 'Fortress Europe' concept a decade ago, little is now heard of it. Primitive Europeans who see the EU as a bastion against the Muslim and Slavic hordes are for the most part seen as cranks, though not wholly without influence. The EU signed the Uruguay Round despite much heart-searching in France. The protective textiles and agricultural regimes are, very slowly and grudgingly, being dismantled. Attempts to create 'strategic industries' at European level have been shelved except in civil aviation. The Union has, again slowly and grudgingly, been widened from 6 to 9 to 12 to 15 members and within a decade should reach around 24 members. Fears that the inherently discriminatory nature of European integration (and the EU's preferential arrangements with African, Caribbean and Pacific, Mediterranean and other countries) would act as a fundamental obstacle to global integration have so far proved largely unfounded.

Despite some threats and important reservations, therefore, the principle of non-discrimination remains essentially intact and a unifying principle behind rules for global competition.

2. *National treatment* As globalization has increasingly emphasized foreign direct investment over trade, the principles of trade liberalization have had to be recast to reflect the different character of FDI. Cross-

border capital flows impinge only indirectly on the traditional mechanisms of customs administration and border controls. 'Free trade', and non-discrimination, in FDI terms essentially mean access to foreign investors on the basis of equality with domestic firms. Such an idea challenges practices which were, until recently, commonplace. In the 1960s and 1970s there was a passionate debate in the UK, one of the most liberal of economies, about the merits of allowing foreign, particularly Japanese, companies to invest in automobile and TV manufacture (a symbolic end to this argument occurred when Japanese company managers appeared at Buckingham Palace in top hats and tails to receive the Order of the British Empire 'for services to British exports'). The US has also largely accepted foreign investment on an equal basis, despite some exceptions such as shipping. France initially fiercely resisted foreign investment but now welcomes it actively, except in some sensitive areas such as the mass media. By contrast, while a few foreign companies have operated in Japan for many years (e.g. Showa Shell), acceptance is still slow and difficult. Many developing countries (India, Brazil, China, Mexico) now allow foreign investment but usually on a restricted basis. There are only a few countries where foreigners enjoy truly 'national' treatment across the board – as was shown when all major countries filed lists of exemptions during the aborted negotiations for a Multilateral Agreement on Investment (MAI) within the OECD in 1998. But the principle is increasingly accepted and is being applied in sectoral negotiations (for instance, in financial services and telecoms).

The next major step in the development of the WTO will probably be a stronger set of rules – going beyond the TRIMS and TRIPS and the limited WTO agreement on services – governing foreign investment and entrenching the principle of national treatment within the regulations of the host country. However, there are some potentially serious problems ahead which have already been trailed in the MAI negotiations (Henderson, 1999). If host countries give foreign and domestic companies equal treatment some will see this as opening up their domestic practices – and the activities of local government – to the risk of legal challenge by foreign companies. The latter could argue that, for example, labour and environment practices are discriminatory (if, for example, the foreign company is dominant within one sector and carries a large regulatory burden). There may also be a clash between attempts to make companies subject to home country regulations (e.g. tax or anti-monopoly action or anti- corruption activity) and host country regulations which are different or even contradictory.

A further problem is that in some cases policy has shifted too dramatically from hostility to foreign investment to lavish and costly incentives, i.e. to discrimination in favour of foreign companies. Many governments now appreciate that one area in which, even in a globalized world, they can make a difference is in ensuring their economies are attractive to foreign investment. The shift in the style of UK regional policy in the 1980s towards providing an attractive environment for inward investment has radically transformed the economy of South Wales. Ireland, Scotland, and Portugal and other European economies seemingly doomed to wither on the periphery have flourished under the influence of inward investment. There is a growing understanding of the common ingredients: due legal process for dispute settlement; speedy procedures; economic stability; efficient communications infrastructure; an educated, well-trained workforce; moderate corporate taxation. But some governments go further, out of over-eagerness or desperation, offering special tax incentives and subsidies, explicit or hidden. With few exceptions competition for investment can be a largely zero-sum game overall, impoverishing governments in the process. This, in turn, suggests a need for rules, at regional and global level, limiting state aid and investment incentives both on grounds of non-discriminatory treatment between investors and to counter the negative externality of competitive subsidization.

Lastly, many developing countries now accept in practice the broad idea of treating foreign companies on an equal, national basis but are reluctant to concede the principle without reciprocal national treatment for labour as well as capital. Why should a UK bank, say, have parity with an Indian bank in India but an Indian service provider (a nurse, a computer programmer, a banker, or a dustman) not have parity with a British worker in Britain? There is no intellectual or moral basis for refusing national treatment of labour, as the South Asian countries, notably India, keep pointing out in services negotiations. The reason it is resisted relates to the domestic politics of Western countries. Governments believe that they cannot concede the principle of freer immigration even if it is strictly limited to negotiated categories of contract workers. Serious anomalies are thereby being created: a Western computer software company will expect national treatment in India (to stick with the Indian example), but a freelance Indian computer software engineer would not expect to receive national treatment in the West; an Indian nurse would not expect national treatment in most Western countries, even if his or her qualifications were accepted, but a Western medical company would now expect national treatment in India. This inconsistency threatens to become an increasingly sore point in international trade relations, and as populous, poor, countries grow in importance in the international economy – India, the Philippines, Pakistan, China, Mexico, Colombia – they will increasingly press for action to address the lacuna in global governance in relation to labour migration. Creating a set of agreed global rules for foreign investment within the WTO presents major obstacles. But, without one, friction over different national rules will grow. Foreign investment rules are a key building block in global rules for competition.

Creating global infrastructure and networks

International integration requires not just competition but international public goods such as infrastructure, networks and standards of safety. A well-developed structure already exists for providing these international public goods in traditional fields such as shipping, aviation and fixed-line telephony. What is far much less well developed so far is a structure – a set of rules and institutions – for the international exchange of information.

There are few issues in international economic policy more important now than the way in which a global information infrastructure will be created and managed. President Clinton's ringing call for 'free trade in cyberspace' has the double merit of anticipating a major new set of international policy questions and encapsulating a clear and broadly attractive message in a sound-bite. What it obscures, however, is the lack of consensus, to date, on how an appropriate balance of regulation and competition is to be struck in 'cyberspace'. This debate affects several specific issues, notably the management of cross-border physical networks (telecoms, mainly), the management of the Internet network and controls over content.

Much of the work to establish a clear set of rules for information infrastructure has been undertaken in the context of multilateral negotiations (over and above EU-level negotiations) on the telecommunications industry which is the main carrier for the Internet as well as more conventional traffic. The industry has been transformed within a decade from one dominated by state-owned monopolies to one – increasingly – of competing and often private suppliers. It has changed also from one where international relations revolved around the physical interconnection and standards compatibility of national systems, and trade was conducted at negotiated prices determined by diplomats and bureaucrats, to something approaching a market (Cable and Distler, 1995).

Reflecting these changes, international 'trade' in telecoms has become a major issue within the WTO, as we discussed in Chapter 3. The new WTO agreement embodies key principles governing global competition. These include non- discrimination, and national treatment whereby foreign telecom companies have market access and can compete on a basis of equality with domestic private and state companies. The EU, to its credit, has resisted pressure from the US for an exclusive club of like-minded countries which offer reciprocal concessions and has insisted on MFN principles, holding open the door to countries which have only just begun to grasp what telecoms liberalization involves. The agreement also emphasizes transparency, so as to make explicit the technical barriers to interconnection which can frustrate new entrants and to lay bare the disparity between costs and monopoly prices.

But new problems are emerging which are not fully encompassed by the telecoms agreement. The creation of large strategic alliances among telecoms providers raises the question of how meaningful competition – contestable markets – will be created at a global level in the absence of a global agreement on competition policy. The present system of inter-nationally negotiated charges agreed between national telecom companies is breaking down, as a result of cut-price call-back services and other forms of arbitrage. The question then arises as to how to progress towards market, but non-predatory, prices in a semi-regulated, semi-monopolistic world. A further problem is to how to regulate trade in 'bads', for instance the proliferation of telephone pornography from loosely regulated centres such as Guyana.

In addition there is a growing list of international regulatory issues concerning the Net (a looser and less technical concept than the Internet that encompasses all the different aspects of networked computers contributing to digital traffic over the telecommunications system). International trade involving selling via email is proliferating as part of a growth in numbers of users doubling every year – from an estimated 8.5 million in 1995 to over 140 million by 2000 (OECD) – though 80 per cent of this trade so far is within the US. The evolution of a system at such speed and enjoying virtually unrestricted and cheap global com-munications owes much to self-regulation by bodies such as the Internet Engineering Task Force.

The question now is whether to allow continued growth within a framework of self-regulation or to build in some regulatory controls. The former approach, adopted by the Clinton administration, provides a framework within which 'free trade' can operate in cyberspace. It argues that solutions to many of the technical problems currently limiting large-scale commercial use of the Net – establishing trust or enforcement mechanisms for making impersonal long-distance payments; or the development of cheap, speedy, easy-to-use, interfaces and guides to the Net's services – are more likely to be thrown up by competition and innovation by firms rather than through more ponderous government agreements on standards. Many of the key ideas for a working commercial infrastructure are, in fact, already evolving very rapidly in the market-place. The aim of an international – WTO – agreement would be to let this happen without arbitrary and discriminatory intervention and restrictions on trade by governments.

Unregulated anarchy is, however, as unlikely to facilitate the development of the Net as excessive regulation. There are areas where public intervention, at a global level, may be necessary. First, there are specific regulatory problems (such as agreed coding for site references) which have to be agreed in the same way as telephone codes. At present these are being negotiated through an uneasy mixture of private (US) groups and (European) governments which have different philosophies about how public goods should be delivered.

A second problem area relates to the establishment of information property rights. Information has interesting properties as a commodity. It is, according to Albert Bressand of Prométhée, 'sticky, tricky and leaky': once transferred it cannot be returned; it can be manipulated; and, above all, it leaks profusely to lucky beneficiaries, or pirates. The principle of protecting property rights is already enshrined in the GATT TRIPS agreement but the special problems of information copyright and other property protection (to permit charging and payment) have to be resolved.

Third, there are big differences in approach in relation to data protection. The US relies on self-regulation but the Europeans are anxious to stop the export of data on individuals to countries with weak data protection laws.

Another potentially divisive issue is taxation. Governments will understandably resist a demolition of their tax base thought the Internet (as sales are channelled to the lowest VAT/sales tax source). Yet trade will be distorted if instantaneous cross-border payment transactions are held up for long periods by customs officials with the computing equivalent of abacuses. So far US pressure has led to agreement that there should be no new tariffs on email transactions and no discriminatory taxes against email commerce. In practice, however, governments will gradually have to rely more on taxes which cannot be moved or hidden, such as property or (most kinds of) consumption.

Fifth, there are potentially serious problems of monopoly – as in telecommunications. At the moment the risk appears minimal since there is a wide range of telecoms and content providers jostling to operate on the Net and to provide solutions to problems. It is, however, possible that big and monopolistic firms will benefit most from early entry advantages and proprietary systems (as Microsoft has done). The US Justice Department is currently acting for the world in its action against Microsoft. But in the longer term this case underlines the importance of having a framework for competition policy at a global level within the WTO.

Lastly – and politically most sensitive – there are worries about freedom of trade in information content. The issue has been highlighted by the attempts of the US Congress to outlaw pornography in cyberspace (later overruled as unconstitutional by the Supreme Court). A variety of governments have already woken up to the alarming idea that the Net can transmit subversive ideas: these include China (which is trying to monitor users and control access) and Singapore (whose heavy-handed reaction has resulted in Microsoft and other companies preferring Malaysia as a site for Asian 'superhighway' development); and no doubt a committee of mullahs in Qom is surveying the material to which Iranians are potentially exposed. Freedom of trade offers a cornucopia of choice to libertarians but it also offers protective remedies. Freer trade in blocking devices will provide cheap, self-policing, mechanisms for families or groups of users who choose to be protected from offensive material. Similarly trade in encryption devices offers products both to those who work to protect commercial and state secrets and to those who want to crack them.

The issues raised here will move to the top of the international economic policy agenda as trade comes to be transmitted increasingly through flows of electrons rather than molecules (i.e. bulk traffic). There is some recognition of the issue in the US and the EU. There is, however, an enormous gulf in understanding between countries and interest groups as to what is involved. Since over 50 per cent of Internet and 80 per cent of email trade are in the US, global regulation is so far largely an extension of US practice and philosophy, which is liberal and self-regulating. No other party except the EU, which has a somewhat bureaucratic approach to those problems, and, marginally, Japan is in a position to make a serious contribution to the global regulatory debate. There is a growing political problem here: how to create multilateral rules, based essentially on US experience and leadership, which the rest of the world will willingly buy into.

The commons

Networks and standards are among a set of international public goods requiring cooperative solutions. The 'global commons' are another: the oceans outside territorial limits, the atmosphere (and climate), space, Antarctica. These present a special kind of economic problem in that they are a form of public good subject to degradation from over-use. Like other truly public goods – a lighthouse, for example – they cannot be provided commercially since it is not possible to stop users enjoying their benefits free of charge. But, unlike lighthouses, the commons can be destroyed if private individuals or companies or governments over-use them, as they will without regulation. They can only be sustained by agreed, cooperative, rules controlling access.

The heightened level of economic activity implicit in globalization is exerting growing pressure on the commons. Fish stocks and yields are actually declining in some major oceanic fisheries. Carbon and other emissions are changing the atmospheric mix with incalculable, but probably negative, consequences for future generations. It is not in the interests of any individual firm, or country, acting in isolation to exercise restraint, so few do.

There is, however, a broad awareness of the problem and cooperative institutions are evolving to deal with it: the Antarctic Treaty, a self-electing club of governments which suspends territorial claims and restricts access to countries with purely scientific motives and a capacity to pursue them; regional fisheries agreements allocating or auctioning fishery rights within sustainable ceilings; ocean dumping conventions; the ocean floor provisions of the Law of the Sea (which sets the conditions – yet to be tested – for commercial mining); the allocation of sites in the geostationary orbit for satellites and of frequency bands for long-distance media transmission; and controls over the production of substances such as CFCs which threaten a common global environmental resource.

All of these arrangements involve a genuine sharing of sovereignty. And it is perhaps not yet fully appreciated how far cooperation has developed, and must further develop, if globalization is not to be anarchic and destructive. An agreement on climate change, above all, will test governments' willingness to share sovereignty. This process can happen either through mutually agreed rules of cooperation or through supranational authority or, probably, both.

Chapter 5

Improving the processes

A central problem of global governance is that however far and fast international economic integration proceeds, political authority remains vested in national governments and national politicians. There is, arguably, an embryonic global politics in the various transnational pressure groups – Amnesty, Greenpeace, the World Council of Chambers of Commerce, the Red Cross – that increasingly, and with considerable effect, demand to be heard on international trade and investment issues. While most of these bodies have mastered global communications to serve their own ends, all but a few are loosely federated bodies or (like multilateral companies) heavily dominated by senior management from their countries of origin. Politics remains essentially national in character.

The demand for increasingly far-reaching global (or regional) economic governance to promote stability, rules for competition or infrastructure collides with national politics in several ways. First, traditional multilateral institutions, notably the UN, have long been dominated by their member governments to the extent that they lack internal cohesion and professionalism and any capacity for independent action; while those supranational bodies with real operational freedom – the IMF, the World Bank, the World Trade Organization, the European Commission – all face challenges to their legitimacy. Second, attempts to widen the scope of multilateral agreements – the MAI, NAFTA, GATT, WTO – have all run the gauntlet of hostile pressure groups and it is doubtful whether future initiatives such as a Congressional 'fast track' would get very far. Bodies, moreover, which require funding from governments – notably the Bretton Woods institutions – are always prey to battles over contributions in the absence of automatic mechanisms. Third, there is a difficult international relations problem in securing agreement among a large number of states which differ greatly in size and status and have varying commitments to openness and to cooperation.

Within those general concerns there are specific political obstacles to global integration which have to be addressed if the system is not to fragment.

Integrating the big new players

Globalization has hitherto been most widely experienced in countries with good communications infrastructure or liberal trade and payments regimes which have participated in the rules-based systems of the Western world. Intergovernmental decision-making is still dominated by the main Western economies. One major and influential change, however, has been the market liberalization taking place in the non-OECD world and particularly in the big countries of Asia (China, India, Korea, Indonesia) in eastern Europe and the former USSR, and in Latin America. The recent financial turmoil in Southeast Asia and Russia is a considerable setback but, inexorably, the centre of gravity of the world economy has been shifting.

The implications for globalization are several. First, the combination of relatively rapid market growth and policy liberalization means that a high proportion of new investment opportunities for internationally mobile firms are in the non-OECD world, particularly in Asia, eastern Europe and Latin America. The attraction is primarily market demand growth and access to new markets. But raw material resources in Russia and low labour costs in parts of India, combined with high education levels, and the opening up to foreign investors of hitherto protected sectors such as mining and financial services, are added attractions for investors. Entry is not always easy or straightforward or profitable; the opaque procedures, nationalist suspicions and erratic policy changes in China or India or Brazil are a considerable deterrent to the faint-hearted. Nonetheless growing numbers of companies, big and medium-sized, are investing there. If there are to be meaningful global rules for competition, covering investment as well as trade, these countries have to be party to them.

Indeed, the major non-OECD countries – China and India especially but also Brazil, Korea, Mexico and Russia – are now major players in the global economy. On a purchasing power parity basis, China is the world's second biggest economy and India the fifth (see Figure 5.1).

Figure 5.1: G10 GDP at purchasing power parity rate

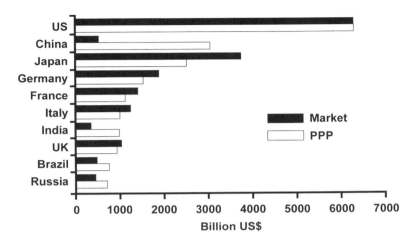

*Source:*Author based on World Bank data.

Their importance in world trade, financial markets and investment lags a long way behind but is growing. Their marginalization in terms of the world economy is historically an anomaly in any event; until the early nineteenth century India and China were among the world's foremost trading economies and, before long, will almost certainly regain that status (Maddison, 1995). As their importance grows, these countries will expect (and be expected) to play a commensurate role in international economic governance. This issue is already being faced in the context of Chinese and Russia admission to the WTO and the pressure on India to liberalize its trade regime. At stake are rules not merely governing trade, important though that is, but foreign investment and intellectual property too. The issues are far from resolved.

There remains a risk that some of the major new players will remain outside, and hostile to, the institutions which are currently dominated by the West, creating conflict on both economic and security issues. The risk of this occurring will be greater the more the big new players are seen in terms of threats rather than opportunities. The sense of 'threat' comes in part from fear of competition. In absolute terms the gap in wages (and conditions) between workers in China or India and those of even the poorer OECD countries is enormous and likely to remain so for a generation or more even under optimistic assumptions about convergence.

There has always been, not far under the surface, a fear in the West of competition from 'cheap' labour overseas. (It can be traced back to seventeenth-century riots in London protesting at Indian calico imports, but has been a feature of several waves of protectionist sentiment (Cable, 1982).) But the virtual autarky of China and India for many years rendered the issue largely academic for these giant countries which have the largest reservoirs of low-cost labour. Their reintegration into the world economy has revived the issue, though so far in muted terms.

The economics of trade between countries with radically different endowments of labour has been discussed already. Those who are not persuaded of the merits of mutual exchange based on comparative advantage tend to focus their hostility on China, and, to a lesser extent, India because they resent what is seen as a lack of reciprocal market access. That hostility is likely to grow unless the big non-OECD, as well as OECD, countries open their economies in turn.

Various mechanisms have been considered to involve governments of these key non-OECD countries more in global economic decision-making: widening the G7/G8; creating an Economic Security Council in the UN; rapid incorporation of China, and also Russia, in the WTO; and an enlarged role for the IMF's Interim Committee. These mechanisms are less important than a recognition that no advantage is served by marginalizing increasingly important countries.

There is a separate problem with large numbers of countries, mainly in Africa, which can be described as weak states and which are largely excluded from globalization not by choice but by poverty, political instability and poor infrastructure. One of the dangers of global governance through exclusive clubs or private self-regulatory systems is that these countries are forgotten. One of the key functions of inclusive bodies such as the WTO, the Bretton Woods institutions and the UN is that the concerns of these countries are kept to the fore.

Legality and extraterritoriality

Throughout history, international order has been imposed by hegemonic powers in the absence of cooperatively agreed rules (Keohane, 1984). The Dutch in the seventeenth century, the British in the nineteenth century, the Americans after 1945 all provided a form of international order. It was based on a coincidence of national and global perspectives which relied on intellectual and political leadership and, ultimately, the use of force to defend the system. Despite the relative decline of the US in terms of shares of world trade and production, its influence – including the Clinton administration's recent support for free-trading initiatives in NAFTA, GATT and APEC – has arguably kept the postwar liberal international economic order developing. Hegemonic power is, however, being deployed in a less liberal spirit. One of the main symptoms of the failure of the international system to deliver a universally acceptable, and enforceable, set of rules for investment has been the spread of extraterritoriality: attempts to impose domestic law on companies operating abroad. The issue has mainly arisen in relation to the US, but the EU too has applied its regulatory system extraterritorially, The issue has mainly arisen where there is a security aspect but also in cases involving competitive policy and taxation.

The most topical cases are those that have involved different approaches to sanctions. The US barred its companies from participating in the development of the USSR's gas pipeline system in the early 1980s. It demanded that European companies should desist too or face penalties in the US. European governments (led by Mrs Thatcher) refused to accede to the pressure and threatened counter-action. A similar situation has again arisen following the D'Amato Act which has been used to stop European as well as American companies from making major investments in the Iranian or Libyan oil and gas industry or, under the Helms-Burton Act, to stop non-US companies doing business in Cuba. These actions were an attempted short cut to achieving an agreed approach to pariah states but they have threatened to make international contracts arbitrary and subject to the whims of legislatures and governments which are not party to them. The end result has been to exacerbate conflict between allies rather than cement a common approach. However, the agreement to create a Transatlantic Partnership to confront the issue of extraterritoriality goes some way to defuse the issue.

Another area where extraterritoriality has become commonplace is the application of competition policy. US courts have not hesitated to rule against mergers taking place overseas, by foreign companies, if this may threaten the interest of US consumers. The European Commission recently tried to apply the same principle by repudiating the Boeing–McDonnell Douglas merger in the US on the grounds that it would have an adverse effect on competition in the world aviation market and specifically in the EU, where there is long-standing rivalry with Airbus. The state of California has sought to apply its tax rules not merely to the income of foreign companies operating in California but to their global income. British Law Lords have ruled that the behaviour of UK companies overseas under foreign jurisdiction can be the subject of civil litigation in the UK (the RTZ/Namibia case). The courts of Massachusetts (followed by New York City and the states of Connecticut, California and Texas) have sought to legislate against European as well as American companies which invest in Burma (leading to a WTO referral). In these different ways, unilateral extraterritorial action, by governments or courts acting on their own initiative, is filling the vacuum left by the lack of global governance in respect of competition policy, business taxation or business ethics. If these issues are not confronted through a system of multilateral rule-making, extraterritorial and unilateral action is likely to proliferate, leading to growing friction.

Transparency, accountability and subsidiarity

It is not enough for commentators to berate national policy-makers for a failure to see the wider picture. Whether or not globalization can be understood and assimilated by domestic political systems depends in part on the quality of intergovernmental decision-making. A culture of secrecy or perceived arrogance by international civil servants and policy elites can be seriously counterproductive. Considerable thought, therefore, has to be given not so much to the institutional architecture of global economic governance but to the plumbing. There are three key principles involved: transparency, accountability and subsidiarity.

Transparency

Opaqueness and secrecy are the enemies of an open international system. One of the lessons from the recent financial crisis is that the poor quality of national data – in relation to Mexico; and then about Far Eastern banking systems – was a significant contributory factor in the build-up of excessive exposure and then, because of the lack of early warning signals, panic withdrawals. Another lesson has been the failure of the existing system of financial supervision to establish the full disclosure of trading positions of offshore funds. Transparency, however, will not always help deal with financial crises; if information about an impending disaster is widely broadcast it is more likely to create panic than to reduce it. It has now come to be more generally appreciated that accurate, timely, internationally comparable data constitute an important public good and one for which international agencies as well as governments have a responsibility.

Transparency is also important in market liberalization. The first step in a process of liberalization often lies in understanding the murky detail in many regulatory systems. The most difficult and emotive issues in international economic integration involve regulations which may be minor on the surface but contain hidden traps for the unprepared (or foreign) competitor. The plaintive complaint that 'Japan is different' rests on a belief that all the informal procedures and contacts which form part of the Japanese system are designed to make life difficult for foreigners in general and importers in particular. The Korean and Chinese import regimes and investment regulations have acquired a similar reputation. Foreign take-overs in Switzerland or Germany run up against surprisingly serious hidden obstacles. Indian regulations can be stupefyingly Byzantine, though they create barriers for businessmen in general rather than foreigners specifically. The opaqueness of the legal and administrative system in Russia explains much of the hesitancy of foreigners to invest. Some of these problems arise from time lags in dismantling old command and control systems. Others arise from genuine differences in business cultures, in some of which Anglo-Saxon impersonality, formality, legality – and transparency – are quite alien.

But it will be impossible to liberalize, and establish trust across cultural boundaries, unless regulation is made explicit. In some cases merely making a process transparent is a major advance in itself. Converting the EU's (and Japan's) agricultural support mechanisms into tariff equivalents has been an important step, not least in spelling out to governments and politicians the price that they pay for inefficient farming. The services and telecommunications negotiations have made explicit many previously unrecognized barriers, even if not all will be acted upon swiftly. More generally, much can be accomplished by laying bare regulations and subsidies which stop or distort trade and investment in general.

Accountability

Much of the process of international economic governance takes place between representatives of elected national government and so there is ultimate accountability, though often some way removed from national legislatures. There are, however, two respects in which this account-ability is being lost, to an extent which may seriously undermine the legitimacy of the institutions in question.

First, a significant amount of rule-making is now conducted within private, self-regulating bodies such as ISO and IOSCO (see Chapter 3). These may well create elaborately democratic structures of consumer and producer interests, and provide for cooperation between regulators, but a necessary political dimension is often missing. In competitive markets, of course, the public interest is served by the market, but where regulation is involved one must ask to whom regulators are accountable. Suppose, for example, that one of the consensus conclusions to emerge from the 1998 financial crisis is that hedge funds should be subject in future to closer prudential supervision by national regulators acting cooperatively. This would operate through regulators some of which, like the British Financial Services Authority, are tenuously accountable to parliament but most of which are self-regulating (if they exist at all). Suppose – to take another example – that a self-regulatory approach to rules in 'cyberspace' prevails; this would mean that rules applying to the UK would be set by largely US-owned private operators, the privatized British Telecom with a modest input from the European Commission and UK Department of Trade officials and, possibly, the UK regulator (OFTEL). It is far from clear how the public interest would be articulated in any meaningful way.

Indeed, and secondly, the creation of independent regulators potentially creates serious problems of accountability at an international level. Whatever the general arguments for and against European Economic and Monetary Union there are legitimate anxieties about the accountability of the European Central Bank: anxieties which are both philosophical and practical, should the project meet serious political hostility in member countries. It is for this reason that much more thought needs to be given to how the ECB can develop regular, transparent reporting of its decisions, as well as systems of report-back and greater accountability to the European Parliament. The ECB poses these problems in a direct and immediate way. Similar challenges exists elsewhere for, say, trade negotiators who are some way removed from democratic processes (and – perhaps for good reason – frightened about what democratically elected representatives would do to the trading system if they were more actively involved).

Subsidiarity

The principle of subsidiarity is that decisions should be made at the lowest level of governance possible subject to their achieving their aim. That is, decisions should not be taken by central government if they can be carried out by provincial or local government; not by regions (the EU or NAFTA) if the nation-state is more appropriate; not globally if a regional group would suffice. The idea is based on several converging streams of argument. Philosophical ideas of democracy suggest maximum popular involvement in decisions. Market principles suggest that individuals or other decentralized units can together produce optimal outcomes. Good management practice argues for decentralization. And an understanding of the interrelationship between economic externalities and geography suggests the need to assign responsibilities for externalities appropriately. Within countries, there is usually a pragmatic form of subsidiarity whereby, for example, local roads are the responsibility of local councils, while motorways and interstate highways are a national responsibility, and sometimes there is also an intermediate tier.

While the broad principle is philosophically well rooted – and appeals to basic common sense – it is far from straightforward to use in practice even when properly understood (Feteketuky, 1992; Woolcock, 1996). Many of the externalities which call for global governance are extremely difficult to quantify and are controversial in themselves. There may often be radically different interpretations of the importance or relevance of the externalities. For example, one line of argument is that global action on poverty is needed because, if not addressed, it will lead to large involuntary migration; but some governments clearly do not accept the linkage or believe migration can be handled regionally or nationally. There are some genuine, international, externalities (e.g. global warming) for which economically efficient instruments such as traded permits exist but which cannot in practice be dealt with globally because there is no common understanding about equity (necessary for permit allocation). There are also major regional and national differences in the importance attached to the issue (relative, say, to economic growth) and in the capacity for implementation.

A constant balance needs to be struck between the advantages of transferring responsibility to a higher level of governance on the one hand and devolution on the other. With the former, fewer free-rider problems arise since all states have to share the burden of compliance with a given objective. There are also economies of scale and scope. The advantages of devolution are the greater political commitment and popular involvement especially in difficult decisions, as well as greater sensitivity to different conditions.

In practice, 'subsidiarity' provides soothing rhetoric but little precise guidance. In practice it mainly serves as a useful weapon for national politicians to deploy against the pretensions of higher – regional and global – authorities. It is probably true, however, that if the subsidiarity principle had been applied to the design of the EU a very different kind of animal might have emerged: concerned much less with trade policy (where the GATT was arguably a more appropriate framework for liberalization), not at all with agriculture (a national issue subject to global free trade), and much more with physical transport and other communications interconnections, river management and common rules to make it easier for Europeans to travel and work in one another's countries. But that is to place the problem in a historical and political vacuum. The EU has been created and the degree of economic integration achieved has brought in its wake a variety of powerful economic spillovers which, under the subsidiarity principle, would justify stronger European governance, certainly in respect of competition policy, and probably macroeconomic policy coordination, as in EMU (Begg et al., 1993).

Where international institutions are still in a formative stage it is useful to apply a subsidiarity test. The GATT, as precursor to the WTO, applied a significant degree of subsidiarity. First, it allowed in Article 24, a waiver for regional agreements, allowing deeper trade integration at that level subject to – fairly permissive – conditions. Second, it left enforcement of common rules to national governments which also had the powers of ratification of agreements. But the new dispute settlement mechanism involves a new, supranational centralization of authority in the WTO, necessary for rules to be observed globally. Third, agreements on standards within the WTO have largely been reached in non-intrusive ways. Standards are harmonized on the basis of performance – that is, in practice, product standards relating to quality, health and safety – rather than on the basis of production processes which would interfere much more with the decision-making of firms. The distinction is, however, coming under strain as environmentalists press for minimum standards governing production process rather than product quality.

Finally, the GATT/WTO has established general rules – such as non-discrimination and avoidance of unnecessary barriers – rather than more intrusive regulations. The single exception is the TRIPS agreement on intellectual property which is quite prescriptive in its approach to copyrights and patents. The loss of sovereignty implicit in this agreement (fiercely resisted by India in particular) has to be set alongside the genuine international externality involved: copyright pirating or breach of patents – seen by intellectual property owners as 'theft' – involves a tangible loss to the investor or exporter affected. Such 'theft' is the mirror image of cross-border environmental pollution; it represents a positive externality to the country which receives it at the expense of the producer. But it is clear that these problems were becoming so serious that the subsidiarity principle could not be applied.

These experiences are important in establishing the subsidiarity principle for the WTO which is facing growing demands for action in new areas – labour standards, competition policy, environmental standards, rules for foreign investment, bribery and corruption – all of which involve intervention in issues hitherto considered to be essentially the preserve of nation-states. We shall address below whether these are all genuinely global issues sufficient to justify global rules.

Mutual recognition and competition among rules

One of the problems in spreading the remit of international rules to almost all aspects of competition is that it threatens to draw international organizations into all the 'nooks and crannies' of every country's economic life. The strong resistance to such intrusion even in the fairly cohesive European Union suggests the improbability of applying it more broadly. Indeed one of the factors that led to the build-up of political resistance to a Multilateral Investment Agreement was the suspicion – however unfounded – that foreigners would be dictating national legislation in the social and environmental field. One way of responding to this problem is the mutual recognition of different standards, or rules, between national governments and competition among them. National differences will exist – in regulatory regimes, tax rates and standards. If these differences are not to become trade and investment barriers then there has to be a mutual understanding to recognize and tolerate differences.

The idea of mutual recognition has emerged pragmatically. The sheer time and frustration involved in trying to negotiate uniform – harmonized – standards as part of the EU Single Market led negotiators to hit upon the idea as a 'fast-track' process for rapid liberalization. It gained in legitimacy from a court ruling (of the European Court of Justice) in the '*crème de cassis*' case, that the use of different product specifications to create a trade barrier was illegitimate. It worked well in the context in which it was introduced: like-minded governments working to a liberal-ization deadline and dealing with a multiplicity of product standards most of which derived from peculiar national idiosyncrasies and brand protection. It has led to acceptance that, through market competition, firms can provide more information to people in other member states of the EU to enable them to make informed choices including the purchase of foreign goods and services.

The same approach has been generalized beyond product standards to the mutual recognition of different regulatory systems (Nicolaides,

1992). The logic of the argument would be as follows: why should individuals, anywhere, not be free to choose to deposit their money in an obscure Arab bank, or invest in a security issued by a Chinese collective, or fly by Aeroflot – knowing the well-publicized risks – rather than have governments deciding on their behalf to exclude these options or impose uniform and costly standards on all countries? The examples are deliberately extreme but the same line of argument can clearly be applied to less disparate regulatory systems. There are several advantages to such a permissive approach: the speed of integration, and thus the gains from freer trade or investment flows, will be greater; regulators will be under pressure not to impose excessive rules or procedures which may disadvantage domestic firms (Pelkmans, 1990; Siebert and Koop, 1970); and exposure of rules to competition will provide more information and bench-marking experience. Overall, there is an enlargement of consumer choice and increased efficiency.

There are, however, serious problems about applying regulatory competition too widely and without reservation. The first is the fear that competition may result in a 'dive to the bottom', undermining the response to market failure which was the initial reason for the introduction of regulation. This is in part an empirical question. In practice, liberalization has often resulted in a 'surge to the top'. Where bank depositors have been allowed to choose they seem to prefer banks from strong regulatory jurisdictions. The BCCI provided a painful lesson for those who did not. When the car trade has been liberalized, consumers seem to prefer clean and safe cars rather than cheap and poor-quality ones (the Trabant, for example, has not swept the unified German market). Air travellers seem to prefer to pay extra to travel on BA or Singapore Airlines rather than risk their lives on cheaper but less safe airlines when they have a choice. But the potential for a competitive reduction in standards exists. There may also be common, ethically based standards – an abhorrence of slavery, exploitation of workers or cruelty to animals – which would be breached if particular governments adopt a permissive approach to operating firms. But this raises more fundamental questions about how far it is possible to have common ethical standards between governments and how far it is permissible to impose standards on other societies – an issue to which we return later.

A related problem arising from regulatory competition may be the use of weak regulation and poor standards as a source of competitive advantage in trade or in competing for mobile investment. The attempted use of the British 'opt out' from the Social Chapter to attract foreign investment is commonly cited as a good example. Complainants against such practices argued that they are analogous to the illegitimate use of state aids; in this case the offending government is subsidizing its producers (indirectly) by not charging for relevant externalities.

However, the use of regulatory competition in this way may be desirable. The original standard may be inappropriate or excessive. Low standards may simply reflect the fact that the country is relatively poor rather than part of an aggressive campaign to undercut competitors and secure advantage. And such differences are a genuine source of gains from trade. It is, moreover, far from clear that low standards in regulatory competition do serve as a source of competitive advantage. Successful exporters and the most successful host countries for foreign investors are rarely countries with the most cavalier approach to, for example, labour and environmental standards. Tanzania is far from being a magnet for cost-cutting foreign investors. Yet the existence of big disparities in standards and regimes, created by differences in income, ethical standards or culture, is proving one of the most serious problems in creating global rules for integration. We pursue the issue in more detail in the next chapter.

Chapter 6

The new frontier:
ethics and globalization

Value convergence

The mass media are at the cutting edge of globalization. It is now physically easy to transmit almost everywhere a wide variety of film, news, soap opera or advertising by satellite or cable TV. Apocryphal stories of Indian villages glued to the latest episode of 'The Bold and the Beautiful' or 'Santa Barbara' and people living under dictatorial regimes in China or Nigeria learning about their country's politics through CNN have a significant element of truth. The print medium depends more on literacy and common language but, at least among the airport-hopping elites, there is a shared pool of comment and literature. A parallel development is the falling unit cost and wider availability of telecommunications, permitting easier cross-border telephone and fax communications.

We have hitherto considered these influences as they bear upon the rather arid world of trade and investment. Greater ease and freedom of information flows have helped to create genuinely global financial markets and made easier the more complex aspects of the management of companies on a global basis. Falling transaction costs in information-intensive activities are making cross-border trade much easier. The global spread of advertising helps to broaden the base of brands and further reinforces economies of scale. All of this represents a profoundly important change in economic organization but it does not, of itself, touch the deeper aspects of national and other cultural identities or personal belief.

Yet it is clearly implausible to segregate economics from other aspects of human existence. In one respect at least the spread of information has had revolutionary implications: in contributing to the unsustainability of totalitarian regimes, such as the former USSR. These were neither able to stop the spread of subversive ideas nor to reorganize their own societies fast enough to capture the advantages of information and communications technology. Yet exaggeration is not in order. More economically successful or subtle authoritarian regimes, notably in China, appear to flourish. Even the pariah states and the palpably unsuccessful – Iraq, North Korea and Cuba – seem able to hang on indefinitely despite the widespread understanding, internally as well as externally, of their deficiencies. Their survival may, however, be short-lived in a broader historical context.

A deeper question is whether something which one could call a common set of global ethics is emerging. The issue is far from academic since there is mounting pressure, at least in the West, to build into the rules governing trade and investment, or to impose upon traders, investors and donor agencies, standards of universal ethical behaviour. The manifestations of this pressure are various and often capricious and contradictory but are too numerous to disregard. These include campaigns for economic boycotts or sanctions against regimes because of their alleged abuses of political freedoms: China, over the treatment of dissidents, and Tibet; Burma; Indonesia, over East Timor; Nigeria, following the Abacha coup and the execution of Ken Saro-Wiwa; Cuba; Iraq, Iran; Algeria; Turkey, over the Kurdish problem; Kenya, over multiparty elections; Colombia, over paramilitary police brutality in oil-producing areas. There have been campaigns in respect of labour rights and conditions including prison or forced labour (China and Burma) and child labour (India, Pakistan, Colombia, Morocco). Customary social practices have fuelled other campaigns: abortion (China); female circumcision (Sudan, Somalia); maltreatment of women (the Gulf states; Iran). There are pressures to universalize standards of criminal punishment (Amnesty's global campaign against capital punishment; attacks on mutilation and flagellation in Islamic countries; concerns over maltreatment in Indian provincial jails and by off-duty Brazilian death squads). Animal cruelty has also become an international concern, sometimes provoking greater protest than cruelty towards people, with action urged to stop seal culling, trapping for furs and the killing of dolphins, the last of these triggering one of the most serious trade disputes in modern times. The Anglo-Saxon press regularly inveighs against Spaniards' indifference to the suffering of donkeys and the treatment of whales by the Japanese and the Inuit. Global environmentalism encompasses not merely an understandable concern for the global commons (the atmosphere; the oceans; Antarctica) but for allegedly unacceptable environmental practices in other countries: the Three Gorges project in China and the Narmada river project in India, and indeed dams in general; the cutting down of tropical forests for timber (Southeast Asia) or cattle ranching (Costa Rica and Brazil); the use of nomadic pasture for commercial ranching (Botswana); or failure to defend threatened mammalian species (elephants in Southern Africa; some species of whales; turtles in Thai fisheries). These are all, of course, different issues pursued by different people for different reasons and with different intensity. It is tempting to point to the randomness and capriciousness of the interventions to diminish their significance. But it is not fanciful to see the early groping towards a sense of universal standards of behaviour which transcend government and intergovernmental commitments.

Contrary currents

While a sense of universal ethics may be emerging, there are some powerful and contradictory signals which have to be acknowledged. The first is that almost all of the expressions of universal ethics emanate from the West, and the Anglo-Saxon world in particular, and reflect the West's underlying individualistic values, institutionalized democratic traditions and current preoccupations – be they women's or animal rights or saving the planet. It is difficult to think of any example of the deep-rooted values of important parts of the non-Western world – such as support for extended family relationships or abhorrence of religious sacrilege – being internationalized. So the concept of universal ethics is something of a one-way street.

A second objection to the concept of universal ethics is that it runs counter to the strengthening of cultural particularism. Globalization may have spread Western values and tastes but it has also made it easier for scattered cultural diasporas or mass cultural movements to communicate. The Hispanics of the US, the Arabs of France and the South Asians of Britain can remain permanently immersed in the languages of their homeland thanks to satellite TV, vernacular broadcasting, films and tapes. The spread of Islamic militancy in the Middle East and Hindu militancy in India has been helped by the widespread availability of videos and tapes with inflammatory propaganda. Groups such as the Kurds, Tamils and Armenians, whose identity hitherto remained largely dormant, have been strengthened through improved communication across scattered overseas diasporas.

This cultural particularism interacts with globalization in several ways. There has been a revival or emergence of the politics of cultural identity in many countries, with the emphasis on distinctiveness in language, culture and taste – from the relatively peaceful separatism of Anglophone and Francophone Canadians, Walloon and Flemish Belgians and the Scots to the violent expressions of Basque, Sikh or Ulster Catholic and Protestant identity. In some cases cultural particularism involves a fierce reaction, perhaps overreaction, against universal values especially when they are seen as Western. The application of Islamic Sharia law and the segregation and relegation of women in Iran, Sudan and Afghanistan, for example, are arguably harsher than was traditional practice. Cultural particularism can also act as a brake on globalization through strong resistance to deregulation of media industries (in France and India for example), to controls over the flow of goods associated with a 'traditional rural way of life' (European agriculture; Mexican peasant maize farming; rice-growing in Japan and Korea) and real or self-imposed disciplines on foreign companies based overseas to respect 'cultural sensitivities'. Indeed global companies often find themselves under contradictory pressures: to respect cultural particularities in host countries and to respond to demands from home-country stakeholders to demonstrate enlightened (i.e. Western) behaviour in host countries.

A third major qualification is that what appears to be a concern for universal ethics is often something subtly different: an attempt to impose domestic values extraterritorially on domestic subjects or companies who happen to live overseas. Thus, outrage over public beheading or floggings in the Middle East is largely restricted to threatened Europeans. Efforts to stamp out child pornography and paedophilia in the Philippines or Thailand are largely attempts to discipline sex tourists. Pollution in Nigeria is an issue because Western companies are involved (by contrast, oil spillage and gas leaks on a vastly greater scale by Nigerian state companies or in Russia are largely ignored). It may be that acknowledgment of restraints on jurisdiction is merely practical or tactical but it limits considerably the force of universal ethics.

Lastly, there are cases where lip-service to universal ethics conceals real conflicts of interest. The two most topical and politically sensitive concern 'fair' labour standards and, increasingly, environmental standards. To a degree the aspiration towards universal standards of labour protection and freedom of association is captured in UN Declarations (though these are patchily signed and ratified and not enforceable) and, more modestly, in the GATT (which proscribes trade based on slave labour). There has long been a campaign by trade union organizations such as the ICFTU to make labour standards more easily enforceable, by attaching them as conditions to trade-liberalizing agreements and, to a certain extent, this has already happened in the context of the US–Mexico NAFTA agreement and the Generalized System of Preferences. Western public opinion has been aroused against producing companies or importers suspected of profiting from child labour in the Indian subcontinent or North Africa and major retailers have introduced stringent checks on their suppliers (after attacks on the reputation of the Gap, Nike, Reebok, C&A and other chains).

Far from being treated as an expression of universal ethics, however, the pressures have been bitterly resisted by developing-country (mainly Asian) governments, and even by non-governmental organizations in democratic countries such as Bangladesh and India, representing the groups supposedly affected by labour exploitation. Their objections are basically threefold. The first is that the motives for threatened sanctions are essentially those of disguised protectionism – almost certainly a factor in the campaigns to block Chinese or Mexican exports to the US. Similar suspicions exist over the (rather limited) attempts to pressurize Mexico to raise its environmental process standards in manufacturing closer to levels obtaining in the US. The second objection is that, even when motives are pure, standards should reflect levels of development rather than universal norms since attempts to apply them prematurely damage the exploited rather than the exploiter (for instance, child weavers in the subcontinent whose parents cannot afford to pay for education and who would otherwise be forced to despatch their children into the greater hardships of domestic service, agriculture and even prostitution). A third argument employed is that there cannot be a common approach to labour standards when global labour markets are distorted by the prohibitive migration controls from labour-abundant to high-wage countries which effectively prevent wage convergence.

In practice, there is a range of issues on which consensus over common standards is emerging. No government will try to defend slavery or trade based on slavery. Few will try to defend forced labour or trade based upon it though there is likely to be fierce disagreement over what is 'forced' and over the legitimacy of the application of external pressure. Child labour is even more contentious, although South Asian governments are now more diligently addressing the conditions in which children work and the alternatives (i.e. school), in part as a result of adverse publicity overseas.

Ambiguities, mixed motives and conflicts there may be, but it is not too fanciful to see in the confusion the groping towards a system of universal ethics to which those involved in trade and investment have to be sensitive. It remains to identify those areas where this phenomenon is becoming most developed, most rapidly.

Corruption

The first ethical issue heading towards a global set of rules is corruption. This is because it is one of those areas where international traders and investors are directly involved and have direct responsibility (unlike, say, the human rights behaviour of host- or home-country governments). Giving attention to corruption as an issue also reinforces the current policy consensus towards liberalization and deregulation since most opportunities for rent-seeking behaviour arise as a result of scarcities created by government controls or lack of competition. Moreover, there is no government or company which will actually advocate corruption (though they may rationalize or excuse it as inevitable in some circumstances). And corrupt decision-makers are no more acceptable to democratic electorates in Korea or India or Venezuela than they are in the US, France or Japan. For those reasons, Transparency International has found it possible to build a growing consensus among governments and international businesses that corrupt practices are unacceptable and should be curbed. A variety of embryonic agreements are being reached to formalize collective actions against corruption: an Inter-American Convention (signed but not ratified); WTO proposals for creating greater transparency in government procurement; tightened World Bank procurement guidelines; a voluntary agreement of the International Chamber of Commerce; and a proposed OECD treaty to criminalize corrupt payments and to make companies subject to greater disclosure requirements.

There are problems, however, which arise not from lack of common values but from problems of definition and enforcement. It is not always clear when corporate hospitality shades into dishonest inducement; when commissions to agents are for bribery rather than genuine incentive payments; when honest dealings with main contractors conceal dishonest practice at subcontractor level; when payments to charities or political parties or local community projects are not used for the purposes designated or intended; when a local partner is engaged to secure influence rather than for business expertise or capital. Corruption is normally defined in terms of inducements to politicians and officials but there is a host of potential abuses within the private sector – fraud, adulteration, concealment of safety information, collusion – which may be equally or more serious. And it is one thing to allege corruption; quite another to secure evidence sufficiently robust to permit prosecution and conviction in courts whose jurisdiction is accepted by all parties.

Whatever the difficulties, there is now a strong case for expecting and pressing companies involved in trade and international investment to adopt strict internal codes of conduct related to business ethics and for utilizing the various official 'clubs' and institutions – such as the OECD's export credit group and the DAC aid donors as well as the ICC and other private clubs – to proscribe corruption and to publicize 'free riders' who condone or encourage it – for example, the German government's tax offsets for bribes used to win overseas contracts. Corruption is not going to disappear but peer group pressure and exercises in shame (including Transparency's list of most corrupt countries) will slowly develop a universal set of ethical standards for business.

Environment and labour standards

We have already described some of the contradictions and tensions involved in trying to establish universal rules of ethical behaviour for environmental and labour standards. In relation to the former, a foreign investor who insists upon emission controls in local subsidiaries identical to those of the home country may be improving standards and incurring costs (paid for by local consumers as well as the company) far in excess of what is expected of local competitors and required under local regulation. On the other hand, relaxation of standards could be regarded by critics as 'exploiting' a host country and seeking out a 'pollution haven' (though there is little empirical evidence that such havens have any great importance). In practice, most international companies are more likely to be tempted to opt for a universal high standard for fear of incurring damaging publicity (or because it meets internal professional standards) even though this may result in 'gold plating' and excessive costs imposed on a developing economy or deferred investment. The 'correct' solution to this dilemma from the standpoint of the investing company is not obvious.

The dilemmas involved seem easier when the environmental problems relate to shared global commons such as the atmosphere (issues of the ozone layer and climate change), the oceans or Antarctica. However, not all societies value the global commons in the same way. Many developing countries simply do not attach the same weight as Europeans to global warming issues and will not accept the same responsibility, or costs, of abatement for solving a problem which they regard as not of their creation and of lower priority than rapid development. Thus, China and India are intensifying coal-powered energy development at the expense of controversial hydro power (which has long gestation periods and is weather-dependent) and nuclear power, with its cost and risks. The consequent increase in CO_2 emissions is not regarded domestically as a relevant concern. The dilemma posed by globalization for companies is that home-country stakeholders may take a much more forceful approach to, say, coal burning than the host country.

As noted earlier, similar dilemmas arise over terms of employment. It is, by and large, accepted that when there are major disparities in wage rates between countries, it makes no economic sense and serves no moral purpose to demand that trade or foreign investment should take place on the basis of equal wages everywhere. But while some wage disparity is accepted, big differentials lead to accusations of 'exploitation'; and, if lower safety and health standards are tolerated, claims that life itself is being 'devalued'. An international company may choose to offer favourable terms by local standards – and would expect to do so, to recruit the best staff – but these will often still fall well short of acceptable pay and conditions defined by home-country pressure groups.

What is happening, inexorably, is that overseas investors in low-income countries are assimilating a sense of ethical standards from their home-country employees and shareholders and mass media. This is becoming formalized in quality standards. The practical effect is, at the margin, deterrence of investment in low-income economies and, for those investors committed to operate there, an enclave of artificially high standards is being created. And this enclave will in turn serve as a platform for campaigners to widen the reach of global standards domestically. The employment impact may well be perverse, certainly in the short run.

Human rights

Difficult though the above issues are, they pale into insignificance beside those created by the growing demands on traders, investors and aid donors to incorporate 'human rights' in their decision making. From one major and arguably unique case – South Africa under apartheid – there is now a growing list of countries for which campaigners are seeking trade or investment sanctions on human rights grounds

What is new is the proliferation of issues and the sophistication and variety of techniques being used to apply pressure on human rights questions. These vary from threatened loss of trade preferences (by the EU in its trade preferences scheme) or MFN treatment (the US and China); the use of extraterritorial legislation (the Helms-Burton Act in relation to Cuba; the D'Amato Act in relation to Libya and Iran); or moral pressure (including consumer boycotts) on companies operating in offending countries to quit or to use their influence to secure improvements (Burma, Nigeria, Indonesia). These pressures have become sufficiently powerful for companies to be intimidated into withdrawing (e.g. Heineken from Burma) or to adopt human rights as a corporate objective within their business principles (e.g. Shell).

In contrast, however, to the emerging consensus on the need for global disciplines in respect of corruption, the linkage between human rights and economic globalization is fraught with conflict and contradiction as different stakeholders push and pull in different directions. First, most international companies are still committed to the principle emphasized in the 1970s in the debate over a UN code of conduct for multinational companies: that they should not interfere in another country's internal political affairs. The UN code, which formed part of the New International Economic Order (and was never agreed), which would have made such non-intervention a binding obligation, is still in circulation. Yet companies are now being urged to do precisely the opposite.

Second, there is often a straightforward conflict between the requirements of a responsible employer and corporate citizen – to make a long-term commitment to the host country – and those of a politically correct investor flitting hither and thither in response to the vagaries of particular regimes. This conflict may express itself in quite different behaviour by different types of companies. Traders such as The Body Shop or ethically sensitive portfolio investors will make a virtue of rapid disinvestment in politically incorrect locations while manufacturers, mining and energy companies with big, lumpy, investments will make a virtue of investing for the long term and staying put.

Third, there is often fundamental disagreement among human rights campaigners themselves as to whether the greater good is served by deepening trade and investment relationships with the rest of the world by a country hitherto isolated from it (the view broadly taken by the dissident Wang Dan and the Dalai Lama in relation to China) or by removing legitimacy through isolation (the position of the main Burmese opposition and, earlier, the anti-apartheid movement). Underlying this difference is a deeper difference of view as to the extent to which global economic integration is itself a liberating as well as liberalizing influence as opposed to one which reinforces existing power relationships.

Fourth, there is far from being a global consensus on where human rights abuse is greatest and which abuses merit priority attention. Amnesty provides objective detail and bodies such as Freedom House give overall assessments, but there are genuine problems in framing a balanced assessment of human rights in a number of regimes: in China, which scores very highly in terms of social development but pays scant regard to legal process and political or religious freedom or the rights of Tibetans; Indonesia, where Suharto's regime made great advances in overall development in Java, and was one of the most advanced Muslim countries in terms of education and opportunities for women but which has dealt savagely with allegedly secessionist movements, particularly on Timor; or India, which is a model of political pluralism and freedom of expression but tolerates near-slave conditions among bonded workers. There is also an underlying tension between the Western perspective, which tends to assume the overriding virtues of parliamentary, multi-party, democracy, and the different priorities of economically successful authoritarian regimes such as China, or the many African countries which have experienced tribal civil war and have reasonable suspicions of the divisive character of party politics.

For these reasons, attempts to incorporate universal human rights in economic decision-making by governments or private companies are going to be highly problematic, and it may even aggravate inter-state conflict where powerful states (e.g. China or Iran) see it as an external threat. But the issue is not going to go away and will be manifested in growing external pressures on the relatively friendless regimes noted for human rights abuse and on companies dealing with them to take up public positions.

The ability of companies to influence events is often exaggerated, since in a highly competitive international economy any one company will rarely have substantial political leverage. It will almost always be possible to substitute a local or overseas competitor. There is only a handful of cases – Microsoft is one – where a company has unique access to markets or technology and these have had only a limited interest in countries where human rights abuse is a serious issue. Nonetheless guilt by association means that companies are unlikely to escape pressure. They are particularly vulnerable to accusations of failure to act in defence of local communities (Shell in the Niger delta) or where necessary collaboration with a public- sector joint-venture partner or host government involves a heavy security operation in defence of facilities or staff (BP in Colombia; again, Shell in Nigeria). In this way, the globalization process is inexorably drawing many traders and investors into the politics of human rights and politics itself.

International equity

Perhaps the most difficult of all the ethical issues is international inequality. It is also one of the most pressing since some important international agreements, notably those related to the environmental 'commons', hinge upon achieving a shared sense of a 'fair' distribution of obligations and benefits. The issue has lurked at the back of international relations throughout the postwar era. At least part of the motivation for the growth of aid and development assistance has been an international application of the principle of income redistribution from rich to poor (Cassen, 1986).

The asymmetric way in which globalization has occurred – freeing capital markets but not labour movements (and with continued trade restrictions on labour intensive manufacturers) – has tilted the balance of advantage in a somewhat inegalitarian way; in particular it narrows the opportunities of poor people in poor countries. This is not to say, however, that greater income inequality is a necessary consequence. In many developing countries manufacturing workers and peasant farmers have greatly benefited from the globalization process.

At present, a universal sense of equity amounts to no more than spasmodic acts of private charity, limited (and probably contracting) intergovernmental aid transfers and a vague sense among better-off individuals and countries that 'something should be done' to help sub-Saharan Africa in particular. Despite a certain unease and periodic (usually exaggerated) panic about mass migration and the spread of infectious disease, a set of issues has yet to emerge which will give this dimension of international ethics greater substance and clarity. It is possible that management of the commons – in particular the need for an agreement on permissible levels of carbon emissions – will force judgments to be made on internationally 'fair' allocations, but we are some way off from such a resolution.

Chapter 7

Conclusion: globalization and its enemies

The perspective of this author is that the deepening integration of economies and societies through improved communications and policy liberalization is broadly very positive in its effects and worth fighting to preserve. It has brought in its wake historically unprecedented advances in living standards and wider opportunities for numerous individuals in rich and poor countries.

Deeper and wider economic integration has also brought problems in its wake: heightened exposure to internationally transmitted shocks and upheavals in financial markets; greater freedom of exchange of 'bads' as well as 'goods'; growing pressure of economic activity on the global commons. These require cooperative, intergovernmental action.

For the most part, globalization has been seen as an inevitable change to which societies and individuals have to adapt. But the inevitability and desirablility are not universally accepted. Globalization is coming under attack.

There are several 'enemies' of globalization whose opposition may come from different sources but which cumulatively represent a substantial political challenge:

- *Nationalists,* who oppose imports, foreign capital and immigrants and want explicit preference for nationals. Potentially, economic nationalism is strongest in the big, fragile nation-states – China, India, Russia, Brazil, Indonesia, Nigeria – where nation-building easily takes the form of a common front against 'outsiders'. In each of these cases there is resistance to import liberalization and non-discriminatory national treatment of foreign investment. But in China and India a steady process of liberalization is taking place for trade and capital flows; and more far-reaching reforms have recently been introduced in Brazil and Indonesia

- *Mercantilists,* who do not necessarily argue for inward-looking development but still see the world economy in terms of economically contending nation-states for which trade is a 'zero-sum game' and which seek to promote the interests of 'national champions' rather than flows of FDI (Thurow, 1993; Luttwak, 1994). A significant amount of this kind of thinking persists in the US and in Europe (as well as in, and in reaction to, Japan), seeking, for example, to represent trade imbalances as 'security' threats. The difficulties of the Japanese economy have, for the moment, diminished this world view but it may re-emerge.

- *Regionalists,* who see regional groups not as a building block for a more closely integrated world but as a closed, self-sufficient system. This philosophy inspired the EC's Common Agricultural Policy and has periodically surfaced as a rationale for closer union in Europe (Hager and Taylor, 1982). Regionalism is inherently ambiguous in terms of its effects. Basic theory makes a distinction between trade creation and trade diversion and suggests that the balance between the two is indeterminate. Hitherto 'open regionalism' has ensured that regional structures – in Europe, North America and Asia – are not the enemies of global integration; but they could become so.

- *'Dependency theorists',* who have argued that the best course for poorer countries is to 'de-link' from the world economy. Much of the theory, and the politics, derives from Marxist-Leninist analysis of the 'exploitative economics of imperialism', but it is echoed by others. The overall approach became deeply discredited both by the failures of 'inward-looking' development and by the relative success of countries open to trade and investment. The underlying consensus in favour of openness largely remains but prolonged recession in Asia and Latin America especially would revive the attractions of 'dependency' ideas.

- *'Deep greens',* who reject globalization as part of a general process of economic expansion, geographical specialization and competition which – they believe – works against environmental sustainability and social cohesion. Not all environmentalists (and Green parties) take this view, many believing that economic growth in poor countries and poverty alleviation is fundamental to sustainability and that environmental externalities can be captured and offset within open market economies. But considerable potential exists for old nationalistic prejudices to be presented in attractive 'green' packaging, especially in Europe.

The potential for economic nationalism

History never repeats itself precisely, so the chances of a repetition of the events of the early 1930s are remote. But there are many ways in which economic nationalism or isolationism could resurface (or already have done), which those committed to an open international system should be opposing.

There is a danger that the economic adjustment required, particularly in the US, to accommodate East Asian trade surpluses in the wake of the recent financial crisis and experience of capital flight, will meet a strong political backlash as jobs are lost in import-competing industries. Classic, old-style, protectionism could re-emerge. It would make forceful use of the slogan 'fair trade' to justify selective trade restrictions: sometimes crudely self-serving, when demanded by threatened interest groups (domestic business and labour unions) in the form of 'anti-dumping' action; sometimes wrapped in moralistic language when it involves trade between countries at very different levels of development and environmental and labour standards.

To date these pressures have been contained. The WTO has established a system of multilateral disciplines which is now quite robust; but it is not difficult to see how there could be retrogression. Economic crisis would play into the hands of the protectionists who are politically strong both on the Democratic Left and on the Republican Right in the US. In the EU it is all too easy to see how a period of economic and social strain could attract support for those who argue for inward-looking regionalism – a 'Fortress Europe'.

Economic nationalism is potentially powerful, too, in the major emerging market economies which so far have only rather cautiously embraced international economic integration: China, which still has severe trade barriers and investment restrictions; India, which also has strong political movements on the nationalist Right and Left arguing against globalization; Brazil; Russia; Iran; Saudi Arabia, which, like the other OPEC countries, has stoutly defended its nationalized oil industry.

The recent debate on the Multilateral Agreement on Investment has brought to the surface powerful currents of hostility towards direct investment and a willingness by environmental and labour groups in the West to align themselves with nationalists. Prime Minister Lionel Jospin withdrew France from the MAI talks because they allegedly infringed 'national sovereignty'.

The reaction to the crisis in Southeast Asia has, for the most part, led governments to pursue more open policies. Korea and Japan, in particular, have relaxed trade and inward investment controls. But Malaysia's resort to exchange controls represents a contrary movement, which could be more widely emulated.

For the relationship between the EU and the US, the most important in terms of functioning of the system, it is difficult to see a return to traditional forms of economic nationalism but mercantilist instincts could be channelled into a variety of incipient disputes, several of them very serious. One is the 'burden-sharing' issue arising from the distribution of trade surpluses and deficit in the wake of the Asian crisis, which has left the Americans feeling unfairly burdened relative to Europe. Then there are the long-standing frictions over agricultural liberalization and aircraft subsidies and new issues on which there has been an impasse, notably audio-visual products. There has been a provisional agreement to set aside differences over extraterritoriality but those differences will resurface in the absence of a common approach to international legality and compatible rules over competition policy and tax.

There are also potential clashes over different standards, as applied, for example, to genetically modified foods or different approaches to the regulation of email commerce, data protection and the Internet. The political relationship between the US and leading European states is currently close and cordial, so it is difficult to envisage conflict between them. Nevertheless there are plausible scenarios – say, the election of a protectionist or isolationist US president; or an ideological rift between the socialist governments of western Europe and a US president from the conservative wing of the Republican party – under which transatlantic relationships could deteriorate badly. If this occurred, particularly in the context of a global economic slowdown and financial crisis, it could be extremely difficult to make headway on trade, investment and financial issues. Global rules and disciplines would weaken. And economic nationalism could flourish everywhere.

Chapter 2 discussed the domestic political underpinnings of global economic integration. We are moving to a world where traditional 'left/right' distinctions are much narrower. As long as globalization and liberalization progress smoothly and seem inevitable, the 'politics of identity' is the relatively unimportant voice of fringe protest. Individuals will gradually adapt to a world where they feel comfortable with multiple identities – national, ethnic, subnational, even European or global. But, if globalization and liberalization are seen as failures (as they already are in Russia) and prone to crisis, then more virulent 'identity politics' will emerge directed against minorities, imports, foreign companies and other perceived threats. If that is to be averted, the global system has to work, and be seen to work, better.

Modern economic nationalism surfaces in various forms. One is the suffusion of trade and investment issues with national security concerns. In some cases – US–China relations, for example, or disputes over sanctions with Iran or Iraq – there are genuine security worries entangled with genuine opportunities for mutually beneficial exchange. But the use of national security is often bogus – as with many 'security of supply' arguments or the 'threats' of Japanese trade surpluses – and is designed to provide a veneer of intellectual respectability to protectionism.

Another manifestation is the refusal or reluctance of governments to accept multilateral legal authority, as with the US 'three strikes and you're out' Trade Act provisions on WTO rulings against the United States; or the EU's non-implementation of WTO panel rulings on bananas. But, to a surprising degree, some hitherto hostile governments have faced down domestic opposition to multilateral compliance, as with India's BJP government's acceptance of WTO and intellectual property law. And in the case of the US and EU the most potentially difficult area concerns a genuinely difficult problem: defining the proper application of the subsidiarity principle. Even within highly integrated regional unions such as the EU, or federal states such as the US, there is an emphasis on setting rules and standards at the lowest possible level. And the precise demarcation between centre and component states will always be debatable and fought over as it is in US Supreme Court rulings over states' rights and EU internal market arguments over harmonization versus mutual recognition. Even in a globally integrated world economy a healthy amount of decentralization to nation-states and regions within them is to be welcomed; this is why globalization can and should coexist with a substantial degree of competition in direct and business taxes, different approaches to product quality and specifications, different systems of labour regulation and corporate governance.

National antagonisms can, however, be aroused when there is a break-down in the consensus over where subsidiarity should apply. Many European consumers demand that their governments should be able to act to keep hormones and GM products out of the food supply chain, if necessary by banning relevant imports from the US; the US argues – in this case – that trade is governed by product safety rules based on multilateral (i.e. WTO and WHO), not national, protocols defining scientific proof of safety. German 'Greens' want their government to ban British beef while British beef exporters take refuge in EU definitions of food safety. Disputes of this kind can rapidly escalate.

There is, in fact, no *a priori* reason for favouring – more or less – harmonization of product standards. There are two legitimate but contradictory principles at stake: the freedom of consumers to choose what they want to eat and the freedom of exporters from discriminatory and capricious trade restrictions. But unless the main protagonists can agree on an arbitration mechanism, nationalistic rivalry will be unleashed.

The fair traders

Fairness, like motherhood, is something most of us are instinctively in favour of, so 'free and fair' trade is a slogan doubly blessed by economic and moral virtue. Yet one of the most potent threats to a liberal trading system comes not from nationalism, in more or less subtle guises, but from those who espouse the cause of 'fair trade'.

In practice fairness is used to qualify freedom in a variety of different ways. Trade rules have, in fact, recognized certain types of 'unfair' trading practice: dumping and export subsidization. Rules have been created to govern the use of anti-dumping measures and countervailing duties (to offset subsidies). 'Unfair' trade in this context stretches somewhat further than two long-accepted definitions: the one where an exporter charges less for exports than for the same product sold in the domestic market, and the other where 'predatory' pricing is involved – below cost – to secure market share and a potential monopoly position (in both cases 'dumping' prices are made possible by cross-subsidy within the firm or by state subsidy). The strict definition has often been difficult to prove and may not be very useful when trade is involved with planned economies which do not use market pricing. In practice action against 'unfair' trade on grounds of dumping has been taken much more widely against 'low-cost' competition where some form of injury is involved to competing producers. However, following the Uruguay Round there are now broadly accepted multilateral rules under the WTO which permit, and limit, action against 'unfair' trade.

A more important issue for the future is the pressure from 'fair traders' to widen the scope of trade (or investment) restrictions further to encompass 'social dumping'. In its most extreme form, this treats all forms of competition based on wage cost differentials as morally inadmissible. The argument is simply absurd as it could preclude almost all trade – or investment flows – since there is a continuum of wage levels across borders (which will also fluctuate with exchange rates) when expressed in a numeraire. 'Social dumping' also fails to distinguish between wages and labour costs (which, of course, reflect different productivity levels as well).

In practice, the unfairness of 'social dumping' remains as a form of populist gripe sometimes used to justify the relatively high trade barriers that still exist against manufactured goods from 'low-cost' countries. But it is now more important in focused campaigns against what are regarded as exploitative or abusive labour practices such as child labour or forced labour. These may not have any protectionist motivation at all (opposition to hand-woven carpets from the Indian subcontinent by 'fair traders' has little to do with the vested interests of machine-made carpet manufacturers). The problem is misplaced idealism: misplaced because the cure threatens to make the disease worse. The strong resistance, for example, by Bangladeshi garment workers to demands for trade restrictions in the US and the EU – ostensibly designed to penalize child labour in Bangladesh – was motivated by the fact that the practical alternatives (domestic labour, agricultural labour, early marriage or prostitution) are likely to be worse for adolescent workers. This is not to say that idealistic international campaigning and aid giving cannot be very useful in improving conditions for badly paid craft or other workers in poor countries – through improved education for children, better equipped workshops, and support for political parties and voluntary organizations campaigning for improved health and safety conditions (Cable, Jain and Weston, 1983). The International Labour Organization exists to secure improvements in this area without resort to threatened trade sanctions. But the use of trade (or investment) restrictions to impose social standards in the interest of 'fair trade' will rarely be right (one exception being that of coercive, undemocratic regimes employing or supporting slave labour – a point acknowledged in the original GATT treaties).

Another form of 'unfairness' which features in some demands for trade and investment restrictions is the case where some (usually poor) countries apply inferior environmental standards. The argument is that since the costs of environmental pollution are not being internalized the country allowing such practices may be guilty of export subsidization (assuming that all the output is exported, or that exporters are allowed inferior environmental standards). The issue arises primarily in respect of companies from industrial countries relocating in order to avoid environmental controls. Evidence for large-scale use of pollution havens is scant and, even if they existed, host countries could reasonably argue that they apply a different weight, or valuation, to environmental externalities. It is unlikely that relatively poor countries, as a group, will agree to have (some) Western definitions of 'fairness' imposed upon them (unlike Mexico, which was in a weak negotiating position in the NAFFA negotiations). Nevertheless, the 'fairness' issue is increasingly about more than economics and now includes attempts to introduce rudimentary standards of global ethics. This broader perspective is inevitable, but it is unfortunate that the campaigns are often led by those who are trying to exclude poor people from the process of global integration.

The regulatory deficit
For most of the last two decades, the approach of leading Western governments to the world economy, and specifically to issues of governance, could be characterized as generally one of benign neglect. There have been exceptions: the EU and US agreed to a far-reaching GATT agreement and have carried the process forward with agreements on financial services and telecoms; there has been heavy political investment in EMU and in NAFTA; Bretton Woods institutions have been, modestly, financed. There have also been good, or at least plausible, reasons for relative inactivity. World trade and investment flows have been growing rapidly, supporting global growth. Self-regulatory systems have sprung up to provide global standards for communication systems, such as the Internet and telecom interoperability.

There is, however, what can be called a 'regulatory deficit': in particular an under-provision of some international public goods. If globalization is to be more securely rooted, then some of these concerns have to be addressed. The detailed issues were discussed in Chapter 4. There are numerous manifestos for a 'new Bretton Woods' and other institutional global reforms. The list of ten points below is more modest: suggestions of practical steps by which the rules and institutions governing global trade and finance can be strengthened in the short run to meet market failures without undermining the competitive, internationally integrated market system which has evolved:

1. A stronger global framework for trade and investment within the World Trade Organization incorporating principles of non-discrimination and national treatment, with a genuinely universal membership, including China, and with global disciplines over regional arrangements.
2. The impetus of a new round of liberalization to remove some of the remaining 'old' barriers to trade as well as to address new issues such as 'trade in cyberspace' and even taboo subjects such as migrant workers.
3. A mechanism for actively managing anti-trust, or anti-cartel policies, in the interests of competition at a global level – either in the WTO or through a new global competitive freestanding body.
4. The introduction of an environmental dimension into international trade and competition rules where genuine global externalities are involved: permitting a waiver of WTO rules if this is necessary to implement multilateral environment agreements.
5. A move to incorporate into multilateral agreements some elementary ethical rules, notably to govern business corruption.
6. The provision of a genuine lender of last resort to countries, as opposed to individual banks, affected by contagious crises of confidence – probably but not necessarily through the IMF or using the collective powers of Central Banks under the General Agreement to Borrow. It would be necessary for countries to 'pre-qualify' for such lending.
7. A much more prompt and decisive approach to commercial debt rescheduling and write-offs, effectively introducing bankruptcy proceedings for countries as well as companies into the mechanism of the London Club (and Paris Club for official debt).
8. Substantially increased resources for the IMF and the World Bank to enable them more adequately to perform those tasks – payments support from the IMF; development assistance to low-income countries – which markets do not perform.
9. A much greater commitment by financial-sector regulators, operating on a concerted basis through the Bank of International Settlements, to impose standards conducive to more sober lending practices and to reduce moral hazard in lending.
10. A concerted effort to ensure that the major non-OECD counties – China, Russia, India, Brazil, Mexico, South Korea – are allowed and encouraged to participate fully in institutions

responsible for global economic rules-setting and policy coordination (including the WTO, the G7 and the committees of the BIS).

This list is not exhaustive and each of the items in it subsumes complex and difficult arguments. But the central point is that the market-led, largely self-regulating system of globalization which has evolved so successfully over the last few decades is in danger of overreaching itself. A period of consolidation, with stronger global rules and regulatory institutions, is called for; otherwise the enemies of globalization, growing ominously in strength, will become a force to be reckoned with.

Bibliography

Akyuz, Y. and Cornford, A. (1995). 'Controlling Capital Movements: Some Proposals for Reform', in J. Michie and J. Grieve Smith (eds), *Managing the Global Economy*, Oxford University Press.

Albert, M. (1995). *Capitalism versus Capitalism*, Whurr, London.

Anderson, M. (1996). *Frontiers, Territory and State Formations in the Modern World*, Polity Press, Oxford.

Åslund, A. (1994). 'Lessons of the First Four Years of Systemic Change in Europe', *Journal of Comparative Economics* 19.

Balassa, B. (1961). *The Theory of Economic Integration*, Irwin, Homeward, Ill.

Baldwin, R. (1988). *Trade Policy Issues and Empirical Analysis*, University of Chicago Press, Chicago, Ill.

Banarjee, B. et al. (1995). *Road Maps of the Transition*, IMF Occasional Paper No. 127, Washington, DC.

Barratt Brown, M. (1974). *The Economics of Imperialism*, Penguin, Harmondsworth.

Begg, D. et al. (1993). *The Monetary Future of Europe.*

Belous, R. and Kaufman, H. (eds)(1992). *Global Capital Markets in the New World Order*, National Policy Association, Washington, DC.

Bergsten, F. (1994). 'Managing the World Economy in the Future', in *Managing the World Economy: Fifty Years after Bretton Woods*, Institute for International Economics, Washington, DC.

Bergsten, F. and Williamson J. (1994). 'Is the Time Right for Target Zones or the Blueprint?', in *Bretton Woods, Looking to the Future*, Group of 30.

Bhagwati, J. (1958). 'International Trade and Economic Expansion', *American Economic Review*, Vol. 48, pp. 941–53.

Bibliography

Bhagwati, J. (1982). 'Directly Unproductive Profit Seeking Activities', *Journal of Political Economy* 90, pp. 988–1002.

Bhagwati, J. (1988). *Protectionism*, MIT Press, Cambridge, Mass.

Bhagwati, J. (1993). 'Regionalism and Multilateralism: Another View', in J. De Melo and A. Panagariya (eds), *New Dimensions in Regional Integration,* Cambridge University Press.

Bhagwati, J. (1998). 'The Capital Myth', *Foreign Affairs,* May/June.

Blackhurst, R. and Henderson D. (1993). Regional Integration Agreement: World Integration and the GATT', in K. Anderson and R. Blackhurst (eds), *Regional Integration and the Global Trading System,* Harvester Wheatsheaf, London.

Boltho, A. (1996). 'The Return of Free Trade', *International Affairs,* Vol. 72, No. 2, pp. 247–59.

Bosworth, B. and Ofer, G. (1995). *Reforming Planned Economies in an Integrating World Economy,* Brookings Institution.

Brander, J. and Spencer, B. (1985). 'Export Subsidies and International Market Share Rivalry', *Journal of International Economics.*

Bressand, A. (1998). *The Euro at the Vanguard of Global Integration,* Prométhée, Paris.

Brundtland Report (1987). *Our Common Future,* World Commission on Environment and Development/Oxford University Press, Oxford and New York.

Bull, H. (1997). *The Anarchical Society: A Study of Order in World Politics,* Macmillan, London.

Cable, V. (1982). *Protectionism and Industrial Decline,* Hodder and Stoughton/ Overseas Development Institute, London.

Cable, V. (1994). *The World's New Fissures: Identities in Crisis,* Demos, London.

Cable, V. (1995). 'What is "Economic Security"?', *International Affairs*, Vol. 71, No. 2, April 1995, pp. 305–24.

Cable, V. and Distler, C. (1995). *Global Superhighways: The Future of International Telecommunications Policy*, RIIA, London.

Cable, V. and Henderson, D. (eds) (1994). *Trade Blocs: The Future of Regional Integration*, RIIA, London.

Cable, V., Jain, L. and Weston, A. (1983). *The Culture of Commerce: Experience of Indian Handicrafts,* Lancer Int. in association with the Indian Council for Research on International Economic Relations, New Delhi.

Cable, V. and Persaud, B. (eds) (1987). *Developing with Foreign Investment,* Croom Helm, London.

Cairncross, F. (1991). *Costing the Earth,.* Business Books/Economist, London.

Calvo, G. et al. (1993). *Financial Sector Reforms and Exchange Arrangements in Eastern Europe,* IMF Occasional Paper 102, Washington, DC.

Cantwell, J. (1992). *Technological Innovation and Multinational Corporations,* Blackwell, Oxford.

Carlsson, M. and Ramphal, S.R. (1993). Report of the Commission on Global Governance, *Our Global Neighbourhood,* Oxford University Press.

Cassen, R. (1986), *Does Aid Work? Report to an Intergovernmental Task Force,* Clarendon Press, Oxford (revised 1994).

Casson, M. et al. (1986). *Multinationals and World Trade,* Allen and Unwin, London.

Castles, S. and Miller, M. (1993). *The Age of Mass Migration,* Macmillan, London.

Coleman, W. and Porter, T. (1994). 'Regulating International Parliament', in R. Stubbs and G. Underhill, *Political Economy and the Changing Global Order,* Macmillan, London.

Cooper, R. (1996). *The Post Modern State and the World Order,* Demos, London.

Corden, W. M. (1974). *Trade Policy and Economic Welfare,* Clarendon Press, Oxford.

Cowhey, P. and Aronson, J. (1993). *Managing the World Economy,* Council on Foreign Relations, New York, Ch. 7.

Currie, D. and Whitely, J. (1993). 'European Monetary Integration: What Remains?', *International Economic Outlook,* London Business School, December.

Daly, H. and Goodland, R. (1992). *An Ecological Economic Assessment of Deregulation of International Commerce under GATT,* World Bank (Environment Department), Washington, DC.

David, P. (1987). 'Some New Standards for the Economics of Standardisation in the Information Age', in P. Dasgupta, and P. Stoneman (eds), *Economic Policy and Standardisation,* Cambridge University Press.

David, P. and Monroe, H. (1994). 'Standards Development Strategy under Incomplete Information', Oxford University, mimeo.

David, P. and Schurmer, M. (1996). 'Formal Standards Setting for Global Telecommunications and Information Services: Towards Institutional Renovation or Collapse?', *Telecommunications Policy,* Vol. 20.

David, P. and Steinmueller, E. (1996). 'Standards, Trade and Competition in the Emerging Global Information Infrastructure', *Telecommunications Policy,* Vol. 20.

Dean, J., Desai, S. and Reidel, J. (1994). *Trade Policy Reforms in Developing Countries since 1985 – A Review of the Evidence,* World Bank Decision Paper 267, World Bank, Washington, DC.

Bibliography

De Melo, J. and Panagariya, A. (1992). 'The New Regionalism', in *Trade Policy,* World Bank, Washington, DC.

Devenow, A. and Welch, I. (1996). 'Rational Herding in Financial Economies', *European Economic Review,* Vol. 40, pp. 603–15.

Dicken, P. (1992). *Global Shift: The Internationalisation of Economic Activity,* Chapman and Hall, London.

Dixit, H. (1987). 'Strategic Aspects of Trade Policy', in T. Bewley (ed.), *Advances in Economic Theory,* Cambridge University Press.

Dooley, M. (1995). *A Survey of Academic Literature on Controls over International Capital Transactions,* NBER Paper G352.

Dunning, J. (1993) *Multinational Enterprises and the Global Economy,* Addison Wesley, Wokingham.

Eichengreen, B. (1995). *The International Monetary System for the 21st Century,* Brookings Institution.

Eichengreen, B. and Mussa, A., et al. (1998). *Capital Account Liberalization: Theoretical and Practical Aspects,* IMF Occasional Paper 172.

Eichengreen, B. and Portes, S. (1995). *Crisis What Crisis? Orderly Workouts for Sovereign Debtors,* Working Paper, Centre for Economic Policy Research, London.

Eichengreen, B., Rose, J. and Wyplosz, D. (1996). *Contagious Currency Crisis,* CEPR Discussion Paper 1453, Centre for Economic Policy Research, London.

Emmanuel, A. (1972). *Unequal Exchange: A Study of the Imperialism of Trade,* New Left Books, London.

Feteketuky, G. (1992). *The New Trade Agenda,* Group of 30, Occasional Paper 40, Washington, DC.

Fischer, S. (1998). 'The Asian Crisis: A View from the IMF', Address to Bankers Association, Washington, DC, 22 January.

Folkerts-Landau, B., and Lindgren, C. J. (1998). *Towards a Framework of Financial Stability,* IMF World Economic and Financial Surveys, Washington, DC.

Friedman, M. (1953). *Essays in Positive Economics.* University of Chicago Press.

Garten, G. (1997). *The Big Ten: The Big Emerging Markets and How They Will Change Our Lives,* Basic Books, Washington, DC.

GATT (1995). *Regionalism and the World Trading System,* GATT, Geneva.

Glick, R. and Rose, A. (1999). *Financial Crises: Why Are Currency Crises Regional?,* Proceedings of CEPR/World Bank Conference on 'Financial Crises: Contagion and Market Volatility', 8 May.

Goldsmith, J. (1996). *The Trap,* Macmillan, London.

Goldstein, M. (1995a). *The Exchange Rate System and the IMF: A Modest Agenda.* Institute for International Economics, Washington, DC.

Goldstein, M. (1995b). *The Asian Financial Crisis: Causes, Cures and Systemic Implications,* Institute for International Economics, Washington, DC.

Gray, J. (1993). *Beyond the New Right,* Routledge, London.

Greenspan, A. (1998). Remarks by the Chairman of the Federal Reserve Bank, Chicago, May.

Grossman, G. and Helpman, E. (1991). *Innovation and Growth in the Global Economy,* MIT Press, Cambridge, Mass.

Gulati, A. (1993). *Trade Policy Incentives and Resource Allocation in Indian Agriculture,* World Bank, Washington, DC.

Hager, W. and Taylor, R. (1982). *EEC Protectionism: Present Practice and Future Trends,* Vol. 2, *The Geography of Protectionism, the Community's Instruments and Options,* European Research Associates, Brussels.

Held, D., McGrew, A., Goldblatt, David and Perraton, J. (1999). *Global Transformations,* Polity Press, Oxford.

Helleiner, E. (1994). *States and the Re-emergence of Global Finance: From Bretton Woods to the 1970s,* Cornell University Press, Ithaca, NY.

Henderson, D. (1999). *The MAI Affair: A Story and Its Lessons,* RIIA, London.

Hirst, P. and Thompson, G. (1996). *Globalization in Question,* Polity Press, Oxford.

Hymer, S.(1967). *The International Operations of National Finance: A Study of Direct Investment,* MIT, Cambridge, Mass.

Irwin, D. (1996). *Against the Tide: An International History of Free Trade,* Princeton University Press, New York.

James, H. (1996). *International Monetary Cooperation since Bretton Woods.* Oxford University Press.

Johnson, H. (1974). *The New Mercantilism: Some Problems in International Trade, Money and Investment,* Blackwell, Oxford.

Jones, B. (1997). 'Globalisation versus Community', *New Political Economy,* Vol. 2, No. 1.

Julius, D. (1990). *Global Companies and Public Policy: The Growing Challenge of Foreign Direct Investment,* RIIA/Pinter.

Julius, D. (1997). 'Globalization and Stakeholder Conflicts: A Corporate Perspective', *International Affairs,* Vol. 73, No. 3, pp. 435–668.

Kenen, P. (1965). 'The Theory of Optimum Currency Areas: An Eclectic View', in R. Mundell and A. Swoboda (eds), *Monetary Problems of the International Economy,* Chicago University Press.

Keohane, R. (1984). *After Hegemony,* Princeton University Press, New York.

Bibliography

Killick, A. (1983). *The IMF and Adjustment*, Vols.1 and 2, Overseas Development Institute, London.

Kindleberger, C. (1973). *Power and Money*. Macmillan, London.

Kindleberger, C. (1986). 'International Public Goods without International Government', *American Economic Review*.

Kreuger, A. (1978). *Foreign Trade Regimes and Economic Development: Liberalization Attempts and Consequences,* Ballinger, Cambridge, Mass.

Krugman, P. (1986). *Strategic Trade Policy in New International Economics,* MIT Press, Cambridge, Mass.

Krugman, P. (1993). 'Regionalism versus Multilateralism', in J. De Melo and A. Panagariya, *New Dimensions in Regional Integration*, CEPR, London.

Krugman, P. (1994a). 'Does Third World Growth Hurt First World Prosperity?', *Harvard Business Review,* July/August, pp. 113–21.

Krugman, P. (1994b). 'The Myth of Asia's Miracle', *Foreign Affairs*, November/December, pp. 63–75.

Krugman, P. (1995). *Growing World Trade: Causes and Consequences.* Brooking Papers on Economic Activity, No. 1.

Krugman, P. and Lawrence, R. (1993). *Trade, Jobs and Wages,* NBER Working Paper 4478, Washington, DC.

Lang, T. and Hines, C. (1993). *The New Protectionism*, Earthscan Publications, London.

La Porta, A. and Lopez de Silanes, F. (1998). *Creditor Rights*, Harvard University Press, Cambridge, Mass.

Lardy, N. (1992). *Foreign Trade and Reform in China 1978–9,* Cambridge University Press.

Lardy, N. (1994). *China and the World Economy,* Institute for International Economics, Washington, DC.

Laussel, D., Montet, C. and Feissole, A. (1988). 'Optimum Trade Policy under Oligopoly', *European Economic Review*.

Lawrence, R. (1994). *Trade Multinationals and Labour,* Working Paper 4836, NBER, Washington, DC.

Lawrence, R. and Slaughter, M. (1993). 'Trade and Wages: Giant Sucking Sound or Small Hiccup?, in *Brookings Papers on Economic Activity* (Microeconomics), Washington, DC.

Learner, E. (1996). 'Wage Inequality from International Competition and Technological Change', *American Economic Review 86.*

Leibenstein, J. (1966). 'Alternative Efficiency versus x Efficiency', *American Economic Review*.

Lever, H. (1984). Reports of Commonwealth Expert Group, Commonwealth Secretariat.

Little, I., Skitovsky, T. and Scott, M. (1990). *Industry and Trade in Some Developing Countries: A Comparative Study,* OECD Management Centre, Oxford University Press.

Luttwak, E. (1994). 'Where Are the Great Powers?', *Foreign Affairs,* July/August.

Maddison, A. (1995). *Monitoring the World Economy 1820–1992,* Development Centre Studies, OECD, Paris.

Mathieson, D., Richards, S. and Sharma, A. (1998). 'Financial Crises in Emerging Markets', *Finance and Development,* Vol. 35, No. 4.

McKinnon, R. (1988). 'Monetary and Exchange Rate Policies for International Stability: A Proposal', *Journal of Economic Perspectives,* Winter.

Miller, M. and Zhang, L. (1996). *A Bankruptcy Procedure for Sovereign States,* Department of Economics, Warwick University.

Mundell, R. (1961). 'The Theory of Optimum Currency Areas', *American Economic Review.*

Nicolaides, P. (1992). 'Competition Among Rules', *World Competition: Law and Economics Review,* December.

O'Brien, R. (1992). *Global Financial Interpretation: The End of Geography,* RIIA/Pinter, London.

OECD (1997). Working Party on Trade, International Market Openness and Regulatory Reform.

Ohmae, K. (1990). *The Borderless World,* Collins, New York.

Pelkmans, J. (1990). 'Regulation and the Single Market', in H. Siebert, *The Completion of the Single Market,* Mohr, Tübingen.

Portes, R. and Vines, D. (1996). *Coping with International Capital Flows,* CEPR, London.

Prebisch, R. (1959). 'Commercial Policy in the Underdeveloped World', *American Economic Review,* Vol. 49, No. 2, pp. 215–73.

Quah, D. (1996). 'Growth and Dematerialisation', *CentrePiece,* Centre for Economic Performance, LSE, London.

Reich, R. (1992). *The Work of Nations,* Vintage, New York.

Rodrick, D. (1998). *Who Needs Capital Account Convertibility?* Essays in International Finance, 207, Princeton, New York.

Sachs, J. and Warner, A. (1995). *Economic Reform and the Process of Global Integration,* Brookings Papers on Economic Activity 1.

Sahay, R. and Vegh, C. (1995). *Inflation and Stabilization in Transition Economies,* IMF Working Paper WP 95/8, Washington, DC.

Samir Amin (1993). *Delinking: Towards a Polycentric World,* Zed Books, London.

Siebert, H. and Koop, M. (1970). 'Institutional Competitions: A Concept for Europe', *Aussenwirtschaft,* Vol. 45, pp. 439–63.

Bibliography

Slaughter, M. and Swagel, P.(1997). *The Effect of Globalization on Wages in Advanced Economies,* IMF Working Papers, Washington, DC.

Steil, B. (ed.) (1996). *The European Equity Markets: The State of the Union and an Agenda for the Millennium,* RIIA/ECMI, London.

Steil, B. (1998). *Regional Financial Market Integration: Learning from the European Experience,* RIIA, London.

Stolper, W. and Samuelson, P. (1941). 'Protection and Real Wages', *Review of Economic Studies,* Vol. 9, pp. 58–73.

Strange, S. (1996). *The Retreat of the State: The Diffusion of Power in the World Economy,* Cambridge University Press.

Thurow, L. (1993). *Head to Head: The Coming Economic Battle Among Japan, Europe and America,* Nicolas Brealey Publishing, London.

Tobin, J. (1994). 'Speculator's Tax', *New Economy.*

Turner, P. (1991). *Capital Flows in the 1980s,* BIS Economic Papers No. 3, Geneva.

Underhill, G. (1996). *New World Order in International Finance* Macmillan, London.

Venables, A. and Smith, A. (1990). 'Trade and Industry Policy: Some Simulations for EC Manufacturing', in P. Krugman and A. Smith (eds), *Empirical Studies of Strategic Trade Policies,* CEPR and NEBR, London.

Viner, J. (1950). *The Customs Union Issue,* Carnegie Endowment for International Peace, New York.

Vines, D. (1997). *The Fund, the Bank and the WTO. Functions, Competencies and Reform Agendas,* ESRC Global Economic Institutions Working Paper Series 26, London.

Vines, D. and Stephenson, A. (eds) (1991). *Information, Strategy and Public Policy,* Blackwell, Oxford.

Wall, D. (1996). 'China as a Trade Partner', *International Affairs,* Vol. 72, No. 2, April, pp. 329–44.

Waters, M. (1995). *Globalization,* Routledge, London and New York.

Williamson, J. (1995). *The Exchange Rate System,* Institute for International Economics.

Winters, L.A. (1987*).* Britain in Europe: A Survey of Quantitative Trade Studies, *Journal of Common Market Studies,* 25, pp. 315–35.

Wolf, H. (1997). *Regional Contagion Effects in Emerging Stock Markets,* Princeton University Working Papers in International Economics.

Wolf, M. (1998). 'Flows and Blows', *Financial Times,* 15 April.

Wood, A. (1994). *North–South Trade, Employment and Inequality,* Oxford University Press.

Woolcock, S. (1996). 'An Agenda for the WTO: Strengthening or Overburdening the System?', Global Economic Institutions Working Paper 17, Centre for Economic Policy Research, London, October (paper originally presented at LSE/RIIA Conference on 'A New Commercial Policy Agenda: Strengthening and Understanding the WTO').

World Bank (1993). *World Development Report 1993* (also 1987 Report), World Bank, Washington, DC.

Zevin, R. (1992). 'Are World Financial Markets More Open? If So, Why and With What Effects?', in T. Banuin and J. Schor, *Financial Openness and National Autonomy,* Oxford.